Contents

Guide to Hydrothermal Spa Development Standards

What You Need to Know Before Building Wet Areas

Global Wellness Institute

Published in the United States of America by the
Global Wellness Institute
333 S.E. 2nd Avenue, Suite 3750, Miami, FL 33131
Telephone: +1 (212) 716 1205

Disclaimer

The content of this book is for general information purposes only and has been obtained from many sources, professional organizations, manufacturers' literature and codes. The author and publisher have made every reasonable effort to ensure that this work is accurate and current, but do not warrant, and assume no liability for, the accuracy or completeness of the text or illustrations, or their fitness for any particular purpose. It is the responsibility of the users of this book to apply their professional knowledge to the content, to consult sources referenced, as appropriate, and to consult professionals for expert advice.

Editor: Cassandra Cavanah
Design and illustrations: Amy Detrick

First Edition 09/2014

Foreword

There was a time when I technically didn't know what a "hydrothermal" experience was. Yet, like most everyone, I learned I've had many "hydrothermal" experiences in my life—"hydro" meaning water and "thermal" meaning temperature. In nature, in homes, in hotels and in spas, people all over the world are increasingly seeking the combination of water and temperature to positively impact their health—or to simply relax and enjoy.

I have been in the spa and wellness industry for decades, and have been lucky enough to visit thousands of spas and sample hydrothermal experiences in every corner of the world…smoky saunas in the forests of Finland, historic hamams in Turkey, hot Russian banyas, sweet-smelling mud baths in Italy, sizzling Ayurvedic steam cabins in India and fun Arctic ice rooms in Las Vegas—to name a few. And I've loved each and every experience and have benefited from them both physically and mentally.

With extraordinary growth in the global spa/wellness industry—fueled by a rise in stress levels (the number-one reason people go to spas)—these diverse experiences are becoming more necessary, and, fortunately, far more accessible. As spa-goers grow become more sophisticated, they increasingly seek more innovative and authentic hydrothermal options—in their travels, and even at home. The market and consumer demand is strong.

So Many Challenges and Opportunities

But integrating hydrothermal facilities entails major challenges. In other words, if you build it, they may come to your spa—but if you don't build it right, you can face serious problems. The design, the "fit," the installation and the maintenance of all these experiences—from a caldarium to a cold plunge pool—are unique and tricky. So much can and does go wrong in builds for both new and existing properties. I've seen many "fails" firsthand. I've sat in whirlpool baths where the jets hit me in all the wrong places, and one where the water was so shallow, my entire upper body was exposed. I've burned my hand on steam room handles made out of materials clearly not designed for that hot, wet environment—and sat in some where water droplets dripped, dripped, dripped down from the ceiling while I was trying to relax. I've been in so many saunas or steam rooms that were either too hot or too cold, or smelled unclean or moldy. And I have faced dreaded "out of order" signs too many times to count.

Yet when done right, hydrothermal experiences can become the highlight of a spa's offering. They offer unrivaled wellness benefits that are difficult to achieve in any other way. (Check out www.wellnessevidence. com—another GSWS initiative—for the most up-to-date clinical research showing the benefits of these various modalities.) Often the hydrothermal features of a spa are beautiful works of art that are enjoyed and celebrated for their exquisite look. Many a hotel, spa or residence will use a hydrothermal feature as its signature photograph—branding the entire establishment.

Because many of the benefits of hydrothermal experiences are achieved without the high labor costs involved in one-to-one therapies such as massage, they can also be a great revenue booster. In addition, many hydrothermal features offer a social aspect to spa-going that is being embraced by a new generation of spa-goers.

I've also learned about the challenges of getting hydrothermal builds right from a large variety of professionals who are part of the process: architects, designers, interior designers, hydrothermal equipment manufacturers, spa designers, wet area specialists, structural engineers, construction teams, mechanical and electrical (M&E) consultants, and the like. Regulations also vary significantly by region. Too often the wet area specialists that know how to build them are consulted too late in the game.

One very basic problem is that even vocabulary, and conceptual understanding, can be lacking, or vary worldwide. In some places people will call a "steam room" a "hammam," for example. The lack of common conceptual vocabulary is just the tip of the iceberg. Building these diverse facilities requires such precise

technical knowledge: from material requirements to complex drainage or electrical issues—this goes far beyond knowing which tiles withstand high temperatures or what wood holds up best in a sauna.

Extensive coordination of so many design and technical pieces needs to come together seamlessly. It's an art and a science—and a true balancing act. And to do that, everyone needs to have the right guidelines and best practices upfront.

This Guide

That's why I'm so thrilled to see this *Guide to Hydrothermal Spa Development Standards* come to fruition. It's designed to give everyone the information "touchstone" and best practices they need before designing or building different types of wet areas. It's really a 360-degree overview of *what you need to know:* from concepts/definitions; to how to assemble a project team; to design requirements for different types of hydrothermal experiences; to guidance on the right building materials.

This guide is not meant to be a step-by-step manual for building hydrothermal experiences. Nor is it designed to cover all the standards and practices one must be familiar with—there are too many specific regional/national regulations to make that possible. Properties will *always* need to use wet area specialists/suppliers who are dedicated to this "art and science." But it is the first guide to provide a universal bird's eye view of what all players need to know before they build, in order to avoid the specific oversights that will cost money and headaches down the road.

History/Realization of Project

The need for a document of this kind first became a topic of discussion at the 2009 Global Spa Summit in Switzerland (later renamed the "Global Spa & Wellness Summit" [GSWS]), the first time that "Hydrothermal Spa Facilities" became a dedicated session on our conference agenda. We invited anyone involved/interested in the hydrothermal arena to discuss: "What can we accomplish together that we can't accomplish on our own?" The room was filled with executives from dozens of global companies, many of them intense competitors, all of whom agreed a set of hydrothermal best practices needed to be established. As the GSWS grew, it firmly established a reputation for producing quality, third-party research, and prompted a group of hydrothermal leaders to approach our organization about spearheading an industry-neutral research document whose best practices could benefit everyone, everywhere. We accepted, and the GSWS research team, headed by GSWS editor and project manager Cassandra Cavanah, began to aggregate the collective wisdom of the global industry and gather expert input from a wide variety of stakeholders.

The result: the work you're holding in your hands—or accessing digitally—right now. Financing for the first edition was generously donated by a variety of sources (listed on page XI) and launched at the 2014 GSWS in Marrakech, Morocco.

The tag line for the Summit has always been, "Joining Together. Shaping the Future." And this new *Guide to Hydrothermal Spa Development Standards* is presented in that spirit: a truly collaborative, global effort.

A Living, Breathing Project

Because the spa industry, as well as hydrothermal technology development, evolves so rapidly, the mission is to update this guide each year, so that it can be constantly improved, with new ideas and best practices incorporated, and any mistakes corrected. We continue to invite expert information and sponsorship contributions to help make this important project fresh, and ever more robust. It's up to all players in the hydrothermal space to make it work and improve it as time goes on.

On behalf of the current board of directors of the GSWS, we invite everyone involved in building, refurbishing or simply operating a hydrothermal experience to read through this guide first. It was

created collaboratively and as objectively as possible. The hope is there will be many more successful, cost-effective, smart, efficient, effective, safe, longer-lasting, sustainable—and more enjoyable and user-friendly—water and thermal facilities in the future.

It's a much-needed guide, whose time has come!

Sincerely,

Susie Ellis
President and CEO of the GSWS

And the other board members of the GSWS:

Jean-Claude Baumgarten, Chairman & CEO, CREWE Associates; Former President and CEO, World Travel & Tourism Council, France

Emanuel Berger, Managing Director, Berger Hospitality Management, Switzerland

Anna Bjurstam, VP of Spas & Wellness, Six Senses Hotels Resorts Spas, and Owner, Raison d'Etre, Sweden

Dr. Marc Cohen, Professor, RMIT University, Australia

Gina Diez Barroso de Franklin, President & CEO, GRUPO DIARQ, Mexico

Pete Ellis, Founder & Chairman Emeritus, GSWS; Chairman, Spafinder Wellness, Inc., U.S.

Andrew Gibson, VP of Spa and Wellness, Fairmont Raffles Hotels International, United Arab Emirates

Susan Harmsworth, Founder & CEO, ESPA International, UK

Mia Kyricos, Chief Brand Officer, Spafinder Wellness, Inc., U.S.

Dr. Franz Linser, Founder & Managing Director, Linser Hospitality, Austria

Veer Singh, Founder, Vana Retreats, India

Mary Tabacchi, PhD, Professor, Cornell University, U.S.

Introduction

As the popularity of spa and wellness continues to grow—there are close to 100,000 spas worldwide—more people are seeking authentic ways to positively impact their long-term wellbeing. Hydrothermal bathing, with its benefits of improving the immune system, managing high blood pressure and body detoxification and the potential for so much more, is one of the most ancient and proven spa treatments available. This is driving a significant increase in installations both in residential and commercial builds.

The main objective of the *Guide to Hydrothermal Spa Development Standards* is to provide the spa, architectural and interior design communities with distinct, modern guidelines for the design and build of hydrothermal areas in public spas and private residences.

The goal is to provide readers—whether they be spa owners, consultants, developers, interior designers, architects, builders, professors, students or anyone embarking on the study or build of a hydrothermal facility—with a consistent and effective means to approach the planning and construction of these unique areas. More importantly, this guidance is also intended to help readers avoid costly mistakes.

In general, there are numerous design considerations, rules and codes to follow. In addition, there are specific building materials and technologies to consider. The handbook looks at all these areas, plus, common pitfalls and repeated mistakes that occur in the planning and building of hydrothermal bathing areas. And, of course, offers tips, tools and solutions for avoiding them.

This first-ever *Guide to Hydrothermal Spa Development Standards* has the benefit of incorporating the accumulated experience of the leading practitioners in the modern spa industry. Spas around the world reflect the "good, the bad and the ugly" of hydrothermal design and implementations; by reading this book and using it as a reference, you are helping to make sure new builds include only the very best of hydrothermal spa standards.

Modern Build Considerations

There are several overarching concepts to consider during the planning and building process.

- Health/Hygiene/Safety: The standards that have become universally adopted are those from the US and Europe.

- Water Management/Containment: The potential damage caused by leaking water is a big issue impacting hydrothermal builds.

- Sustainability/Energy Conservation: Incorporating these principles into the initial design and build process will ultimately save both money and resources in the long term.

- Health Benefits: Hydrothermal experiences can contribute greatly to a society's overall wellness (reducing stress, disease, etc.). Being aware of these benefits and educating bathers of them will lead to a greater adoption.

This handbook is not designed as an exhaustive guide to a "model" hydrothermal build from beginning to end—you will need to employ specialist suppliers and/or consultants for this. It is, instead, a first step to familiarizing yourself with the key areas, understanding their functions and benefits and getting an overview that can guide you in your decision-making.

Notice to Readers

Key terminology will be explained in the text; as well, the glossary (page 107) goes into further detail to minimize confusion regarding the terms associated with modern hydrothermal spa areas.

There will be references to building codes and other safety guidelines the global hydrotherapy industry follows, but these references are not exhaustive and you will need to consult your relevant local codes and guidelines.

Guide to Hydrothermal Spa Development Standards Contributors

GWI would like to thank the following companies for their contributions and support in making this guide come to life.

Chapter One

Overview of Hydrothermal Bathing

In this book, we explore the world of hydrothermal spa bathing, also known as "aquathermal spa," depending on the use of either the Greek or Latin root of "water." Put simply, these are areas where people get either wet (hydro) and/or experience a change of temperature (thermal).

For thousands of years, different cultures have sought to harness the cleansing and healing power of water and heat—both considered luxuries in ancient times. Access to either was often difficult. This prompted more civilized societies throughout the world to find creative ways to deliver "hydro" and "thermal" to their citizens.

Often the easiest way to do this was through natural hot springs, areas that have always played a key role in hydrothermal bathing. The abundance of hot springs around the globe made it possible for many cultures to take advantage of these sites to construct dedicated buildings on or around them, prompting the concept of public bathing.

The geo-thermally warmed waters that bubbled up from the earth's core not only served to cleanse its users, but "taking the waters" was also believed (and is now medically proven) to deliver minerals to improve certain skin conditions and relieve pain from arthritis

Hydrothermal bathing has been practiced for thousands of years. The pools at Bath Spa, UK.

and other musculoskeletal ailments. As far back as the 7th century B.C., there are mentions of a "spring which contains sulfur to treat disease" in Chinese history books.

Private bathing areas were virtually unheard of in ancient times, so the most efficient means for washing was to gather in these public bathing spaces. Perhaps the best known and most cited examples of public bathing houses come from the Romans—their advanced technology and grandiose architecture (not to mention their geographical domination of Europe and Asia) positioned them as forerunners in hydrothermal bathing. But there are plenty of other cultures that also take credit for the invention of some of today's popular hydrothermal applications.

For example, a highly popular and long enduring hydrothermal treatment is the Finnish sauna. With heat being such a prized resource in freezing Finland, the Finns devised a means to heat a wooden cabin to the highest degrees, causing the occupants to become very hot. Leaving the cabin, sweating profusely, they then used the snow outside to wipe off the sweat and dirt skin—and repeated the process as several times as the need to be clean dictated. This is why, even today,

the Finns typically take a "roll in snow" after bathing in the sauna. The practical reason for diving into the snow is because running water was in short supply during the frozen winters of the north. But the result is a cleansing/detoxifying ritual that is valued to this day and has been proven to improve the immune system and reduce blood pressure.

It should be noted that though Finland is often recognized as the birthplace of the sauna, the whole of the frozen northern Europe was known to have invented similar forms of bathing—for example, the Russian banya is almost identical in design and purpose.

On the American continent, there is early evidence of "sweating" as a form of cleansing, including the use of aromatic herbs and flowers (or "aromatherapy," as it's known today). The Aztec tribes were particularly influential in their creation of two-story wattle-and-daub sweat rooms. In Mexico, the temazcal or "sweat lodge" is another example of thermal bathing; today, you can visit an excellent example of a Mayan steam room at the Chechen Itza site in the Mexican Yucatan Peninsula.

Turkish hamams feature a heated belly stone (gobek tasi) as their centerpiece. This is where the traditional soap massage takes place.

During the 16th century, the Ottoman Empire gave rise to the now-famous hamam (or Turkish bath). There is evidence, however, to show this form of bathing predates the Ottomans and was used widely in North Africa and the Middle East even prior to the rise of Islam. Once again using sweating as a form of cleansing, the traditional hamam became particularly popular before a visit to the mosque. The old hamams of Istanbul boast beautiful interiors including fantastic examples of traditional Muslim ceramic and mosaic art with inscriptions from the Koran often being present on the walls. You can also find fine examples of hamams in Syria, Lebanon, Jordan, Tunisia, Libya, Algeria and Morocco. *Note: The Turkish hamam has a single central "m," while the Moroccan hammam is spelled with two.*

Japan is also known for its extensive bathing culture with an ethic of cleanliness rooted deep in its culture. As long ago as the 3rd century, references to the Japanese habits of cleanliness surface in writings, and, in the 6th and 7th centuries, the rise of Confucianism and Buddhism further solidified the virtues of cleanliness in general along with the love of the ritual of bathing. Japan's more than 20,000 natural hot springs formed the original onsens. The Japanese also developed a form of steam bath called the sento, a type of vapor bath that used aromatherapy elements and included body scrubbing. And, finally, the furo is a bath made of wood long enough for the bather to lie flat; it's often found in private homes.

Another type of thermal bathing—mud bathing—originated in the Middle East thousands of years ago. This form of bathing wasn't necessarily devised to "cleanse the masses," but, instead, was a medicinal and beautifying ritual using the mineral-rich silt of the Dead Sea to treat skin conditions. Similarly, the Ancient Egyptians valued the healing powers of the mud of the Nile delta, which delivered minerals and deposits from the high mountain ranges of Ethiopia.

And then in the 1900s, the French began harnessing the restorative properties of the sea—which is rich not only in sodium chloride (salt) but also minerals and trace elements. Known as "thalassotherapy," treatments evolved to use warm seawater to allow the minerals to pass through the skin, complemented by algae, seaweed and alluvial mud applications.

Benefits of Hydrothermal Experiences

So the origin of hamams, saunas, onsens, etc., ultimately derived from the need to cleanse the body. However, there are now recognized health and aesthetic benefits associated with all forms of hydrothermal bathing. In recent years, medical science has explored the effects the immersion in hot temperatures, and the subsequent transfer to cold, has on the body—and have determined that a key benefit of such temperature change is detoxification. Getting hot and sweating out impurities is important to our health, and experiencing extreme changes in body temperature also increases the circulation and gives the body functions a positive jolt.

The importance of thermal bathing, and the pleasure derived from it, is undisputed and well-recorded over the centuries, but it has only really been in the last 200 years or so that the medical profession has looked into the physical benefits, rather than just the ability to cleanse. In particular, there are multiple medical studies that confirm the reduction of hypertension with use of saunas. Evidence-based studies can be found at www.wellnessevidence.com, a portal designed to help people explore thousands of studies that have been done on common wellness therapies.

Although not scientifically proven at the time, the effect of the heat, and the minerals, along with the social aspect of communal bathing and the hygiene benefits that resulted, combined to create almost miraculous results. Even fertility was seemingly improved—in the 1700s, Queen Mary "took the waters" at the thermal springs in Bath, England while apparently suffering from infertility and 10 months later gave birth to a son.

In addition to the medical benefits, there is the simple notion of "thermal pleasure"—the feeling a person experiences when moving from a place where the temperatures have eventually made them uncomfortable to one where the contrasting temperature brings immediate relief and an almost euphoric feeling of pleasure. Hydrothermal spa areas provide this pleasure while delivering a social and ritualistic experience.

In the modern world, public bathing has evolved from being a necessity (i.e., the only way to cleanse

Japan is known for its extensive bathing culture; an onsen at Hoshino Resorts Co., Ltd. In Hakone, Japan

the masses) to a ritual (and often a private one) that not only helps purify the body, but also one that gives us a chance to take a break from our busy, stressful lifestyles—allowing for complete and utter relaxation.

Modernization of Hydrothermal Spa Bathing

What is a "spa" anyway? Many think the term originates from the Latin "sanus per aquam," which translates into "health through water," while many Europeans associate the word with old European spa towns where natural springs, hot or cold, saline or sulfuric, produce endless quantities of natural water. Britons of the Victorian era were famous for traveling widely to "take the waters" of spa towns throughout Europe, which were believed to have medicinal or healing powers. Another suggestion is that the term "spa" comes specifically from another famous bathing site of the same name: "Spa" in Belgium.

Many of the now-famous European spa towns were actually put on the map over two thousand years ago during the Roman invasion of Europe, when the Romans brought their already advanced bathing culture to the lands they conquered. For example, Emperor Caracalla believed the hot springs of Baden-Baden in Germany cured his arthritis, and he consequently built one of the finest bathing houses outside Rome in this location.

It has often been said that a visit to a spa should be a journey of discovery—not just of new experiences, but a discovery of the joy of true relaxation and of self-indulgence. Spa and hotel developers, as well as homeowners, are realizing more and more that this journey can be significantly enhanced with the addition of hydrothermal experiences.

The ability to rest in the intense warmth of the sauna, to enjoy the benefits of steam bathing or salt inhalation, to exhilarate in a cold plunge, to refresh in the more gentle, cooling atmosphere of a snow cavern, and to invigorate with dips in specially designed hydrotherapy pools without the worry of time, is perhaps the ultimate in relaxation.

And, if between these experiences you can relax in comfort, either in silent relaxation spaces or, more sociably, on heated loungers that may surround a hydrotherapy pool, the experience is enhanced.

Overview of Popular Hydrothermal Experiences

This section provides a brief overview of the areas seen most frequently in both commercial and residential builds, from the hottest to the coolest space.

Sauna

Generally a simple timber cabin with a heat source radiating warmth from the wood-clad walls via heated stones, warmed by electricity or gas, but traditionally by log fires, and normally operating between 70° C and 105° C. Many versions are available, but the most authentic are Kelo log-house saunas, which replicate the early origins of this form of bathing. However, as these are traditionally designed as independent external structures, the sauna has undergone substantial modernization as it has been brought inside spa buildings to form part of a hydrothermal bathing suite.

Steam Bath or Steam Room

Often called a caldarium or sudatorium from its Roman bath equivalent, a steam bath (or steam room) is typically a tiled or stone room reaching temperatures of between 42° C and 48° C with 100% humidity provided by hot steam, which is either created from heated waters in the room itself or, more commonly, pumped into the room using a steam generator. Aromatic extracts of essential oils can be injected concurrently to give the steam bath an added sensory element.

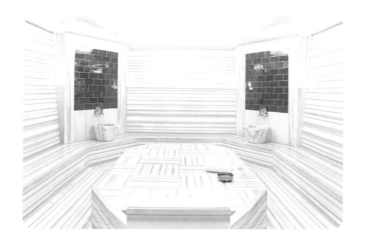

Hamam or Hammam

Also known as "Turkish baths," or Moroccan hammams, modern hamams are normally larger than a steam bath. Turkish hamams have a traditional heated "göbek tasi," or, literally, "belly stone," as their centerpiece. A smaller replica located in an adjacent room will enable bathers to receive the soap massage in private. The heated floor, walls and benches warm the room to 40° C to 42° C with, possibly (but not essentially), 40% to 60% humidity from an independent steam source. An authentic atmosphere is achieved when the room is finished in traditional Turkish "Iznik" tiles and Carrara Blanco marble, although dramatic effects have been created in modern hamams using very different finishes.

Mud Bath

Mud bathing originated thousands of years ago as a medicinal and beautifying ritual—depending on the minerals inherent in the mud, these baths can cleanse, exfoliate, absorb toxins, increase circulation and soften the skin. The bather can either be fully immersed in mud (as seen here), or the mud can be applied by a therapist or a bathing partner.

Vitality Pool

A vitality pool is the generic name for what people commonly refer to as a "Jacuzzi" (the brand name that has become synonymous with pools with water jets). Vitality pools offer a mini-hydrotherapy experience and are typically used where space will not permit the inclusion of a full-size hydrotherapy pool. These pools typically operate at 35° C to 38° C and will have underwater pressurized air and water features.

Laconium

Again a name from the Roman era, this is a warm ceramic room, with a temperature of 38° C to 42° C, in which bathers can relax for long periods of time in comfortable ergonomically designed benches or individual, heated loungers or chairs. The walls, floors and benches are heated to enable deep penetration of the warmth to the body, promoting a feeling of wellbeing and relaxation. Aromas can be introduced via a humidifier to enhance this beneficial treatment and maintain a comfortable atmosphere. Heated loungers are often provided in ceramic or stone (or other impervious finishes) to the quiet spaces in and around the wet areas of the spa, as they are particularly suitable for "wet" relaxation between thermal treatments/baths.

Relaxation Spaces

Once again taking origins from the ancient bathing cultures, these areas were known as tepidariums by the Romans; sometimes smaller, more intimate spaces were provided for rest—and even sleeping—and were known as refugiums. Fitted with a range of different beds and loungers, these spaces are essential to any spa. When allocating space to a relaxation area, consideration should be given to the fact that after bathing in a sauna for 10 minutes, it will take at least 20 minutes for the bather's body temperature to equalize, which is the only time he/she should return to a warm/hot cabin or pool. Logically, there should at least be as many seats/loungers as there are total places in the thermal cabins and pools.

Foot Spa

The foot spa is traditionally an area where warm ceramic or mosaic benches offer a place to relax and be comfortable, while bathing the feet in cool or warm (never hot) water. Feet are especially important in the heating and cooling process of a hydrothermal journey because the small amount of flesh and fat on them, combined with the large number of blood vessels, allow this cooling or warming effect to be conveyed through the body via the heated or cooled bloodstream.

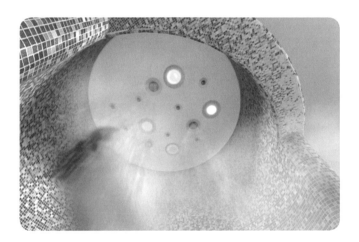

Experience Shower

change this paragraph to: There are a huge variety of showers—cold waterfalls, mists, body jets and dramatic "experience showers"—offering multi-sensory experiences that incorporate smells, sound and visual effects that help take the bather to another world.

Hydrotherapy Tub

Individual hydrotherapy tubs deliver a unique sensation of heat, buoyancy and hydro-massage. Jets can be positioned to stimulate and relax trigger points in the body. High-quality units will massage body zones, beginning at the feet and going towards the upper part of the body, and will have automatic programs with different focuses and varying pressures. Aromatherapy oil can be added to the baths to intensify the bather's relaxation and engage the other senses. Soothing skin products are often used. The natural healing power of mineral water or seawater can increase their effectiveness.

Vichy Shower

A Vichy shower is a horizontal series of showerheads forming a "rain bar" over a waterproof, cushioned table that features drainage on the side for all the excess water. This is a therapist controlled water massage designed to increase blood circulation, hydrate the skin and soothe/relax muscles.

Dry Floatation Bed

Dry floatation beds offer a sense of weightlessness and are used in combination with a body wrap and often include soft hydro-massage features. Because the unit can be stable, manual massages can also take place on the bed, making it a very flexible choice in a modern spa.

Kneipp Walk

Kneipp therapy was founded in the 19th century by Sebastian Kneipp, a Bavarian parish priest, who was ill with tuberculosis and developed this "water cure" to heal himself. Kneipp therapy does not always take place in a pool—in fact hot and cold compresses can be used—but, pools are most common. The Kneipp walk uses a mix of hot- and cold-water actions (stepping through the water) to stimulate the circulation of blood. Pebbles on the bottom of the stream/walkway massage the feet, and the alternation of hot and cold baths stimulate circulation of all parts of the body. There are two walks used—the bather begins by stepping in hot water and then moves to cold water.

Plunge Pool

Traditional cold-water pools stem from the Romans who realized that the surge of blood, caused by contracting blood vessels, which had previously expanded in the hot rooms, was a particularly invigorating experience. This practice is now accepted as a beneficial way of increasing blood flow and can help naturally reduce cholesterol levels in arteries and relieve hypertension. Purists would have it that a plunge pool should be barely above freezing point, but temperatures of 12° C to 20° C are effective. These were dubbed Frigidariums by the Romans.

Ice Fountains, Ice Caves and Igloos

The gentler experience of the cool air associated with the northern extremes can be created by a tiled, domed roof "Igloo" or a "cave" formed in replica rock and maintained at 4° C to 15° C. With an ice fountain inside these rooms, crushed ice can be applied to the limbs gently to selectively cool the body. The cool air allows the lungs and the blood to be cooled from within if the bather practices deep breathing exercises.

Snow Caverns

Using modern techniques to create real snow, there can be nothing more exhilarating than stepping from a traditional sauna into a rock stone landscape covered with a fresh fall of real snow with which to cool the body. Operating at 1° C to 4° C, these rooms are becoming features in some modern spas, as we slowly, but surely, retrace our steps to provide ever more authentic experiences closer to the origins of the treatments we all now desire.

Chapter Two

Project Planning

This chapter gives readers a broad overview of the considerations that should be made during the planning stages of a hydrothermal spa project. It will take a look at some of the major oversights that commonly occur and give suggestions on how to avoid them.

Note: Much of this chapter relates to larger commercial builds, though the principles can be applied to any size project.

Perhaps surprisingly, one of the most significant stumbling blocks in the planning of a hydrothermal spa area—whether it's commercial or residential—is a misunderstanding of basic terminology and functionality. There can be a lot of confusion around what each of the thermal cabins does (i.e., are they dry or wet? hot, humid or cold?) or how a pool functions. Because terminology can differ from country to country, the confusion is often escalated. For example, what's the difference between a hamam and a steam bath? a sauna or a banya? or a steam shower and an experience shower? If the whole team does not "speak" the same language, it becomes impossible to deliver to a client's expectations.

This handbook will help minimize these issues by providing clear definitions of the hydrothermal features that are typically included in a modern build. The reader will find detailed descriptions of thermal rooms (chapter three) and hydrotherapy pools (chapter four), as well as a glossary of key hydrothermal terms (page 107). However, it should be noted that this handbook is only a starting-off point, and, regardless

Spa Flow

When designing a hydrothermal spa area, the flow
of both guest and staff must be considered.

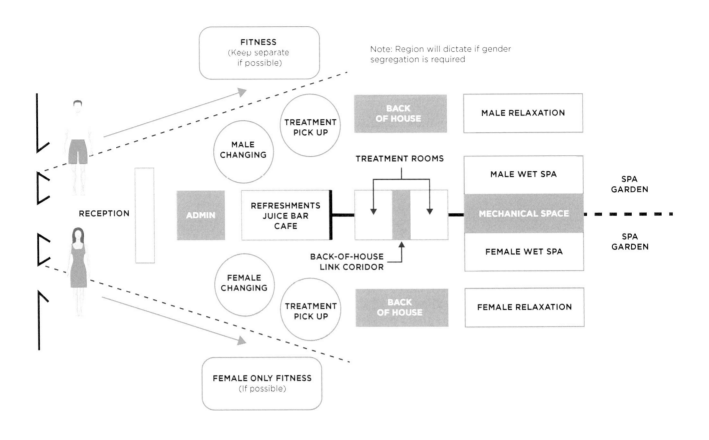

of the size of a build, it is always recommended that a hydrothermal specialist be appointed at the outset of the project. Without a wet area specialist on the team, there will always be a risk of overlooking some very basic requirements that will ultimately end up costing both time and money.

Crucial Considerations

The most crucial considerations in a new build are space requirements and people flow.

A common error is underestimating the space required for the plant room and mechanical equipment. For example, a simple hydrotherapy pool may not look too big, but it requires almost as much space again for the associated plant and equipment. On the other

hand, a Finnish sauna needs next to nothing in terms of additional space, unless it features an automatic essence dosing system, which requires its own plant cupboard.

Consideration for people flow (both for guests and staff) is also critical. Staff should have a completely different flow from guests so they can perform behind-the-scenes functions without being seen, like setting up treatments, gathering used linens and cleaning.

Generally, the way people interact in hydrothermal areas differs greatly from the way they would interact in other public spaces (as noted on page 19 and page 67). It's important to be aware of the need for extra personal space.

Additionally, the intense heat of the thermal treatments means that space must be allocated for cooling off (through showers and plunge pools) and relaxing between treatments. As an example, 10 minutes in a sauna requires 20 minutes to 30 minutes cooling time (of course, in practice, people will listen to their bodies and these times will vary significantly). Space should be allocated accordingly—if, for example, the thermal cabins in a spa seat 15 people, then the relaxation/cooling areas need to accommodate at least the same number, if not more, people. The customer journey through the spa should also be logical and simple to follow.

Key Considerations

- Seek professional advice early—these are specialized areas; wet area specialists are required

- Be clear on budget—a wet area is not a place to cut corners; understanding this at the outset will minimize frustrations

- Know your audience—preferences around the world vary greatly so make sure hydrothermal features are targeted to your audience

- Balance is important—achieve the correct balance between water (pools) and thermal experiences (steam baths, saunas, etc.)

- Don't underestimate space requirements—wet spa areas often require twice the space to accommodate behind-the-scenes equipment and maintenance

- Bathers and staff require different flows—understand who will be using and working in the various spaces and plan accordingly

- Don't forget the plant room and equipment—the detailed plant and technical equipment requirements (plant rooms, etc.) are frequently undocumented in early planning stages; this omission often means going back to the drawing board partway through a build—with consequent time delays and extra costs

- Noise is the enemy—customer relaxation will be non-existent and the ambience of the spa will be severely compromised if noise emissions aren't kept

Common Mistakes

- Failing to hire a spa wet area specialist at the beginning of a project

- Underestimating/ignoring space required for plant room and mechanical equipment

- Lack of attention to people flow—both of guests and staff

- Not accounting for variances in cultures and the types of treatments and facilities guests will want and use (i.e., know your target audience)

- Noise is the enemy of a relaxing spa experience; whether it's a hydrotherapy pool or a plant room operating a steam bath—put them where they can't be heard

- Building with substandard materials that can't handle extensive heat and moisture

- Failing to follow proper drainage and ventilation standards

- Lack of awareness of health, safety and hygiene in every aspect of the design

to a minimum (for example, a relaxation space should not be adjacent to a vitality pool, which can be quite noisy and often generates conversation)

- Water egress is also the enemy—a lack of detailed planning in the materials used, construction techniques and drainage can result in water leakage/damage throughout the facility, which can lead to health issues like mold and bacteria growth such as legionella

Hydrothermal spa builds require experts, such as MEP consultants and structural engineers.

Assembling a Project Team

For a commercial build, it is vital to engage an architect and interior designer, preferably with spa experience. In addition, an operational spa consultant should be a key part of the team. They will help create the business plan; plot the flow of guests through the spa; assist in choosing the products and services required; and coordinate staff recruitment/training, etc.

A proactive client will listen to his/her team's advice, but will also be prepared to question it. It's important to make numerous spa visits, including to spas that members of the team have designed, operated, built or consulted on. It's a good idea to speak to other spa owners/operators to identify critical success factors and things they would have done differently.

A hydrothermal spa based on a single team member's personal tastes or operating experience is not a satisfactory objective for a project. Instead, a spa that meets an owner/operator's own vision, while incorporating industry best practices and unique customer selling points is the desired outcome.

Specialist Hydrothermal Team

Don't underestimate the complexity of the building services associated with a wet spa. Even if the architect and interior designer have been involved in this type of build before, it doesn't necessarily mean they have the detailed expertise required to properly execute these critical areas.

A successful build is based on collaboration between the design/construction team and a specialist wet area team that will bring detailed knowledge of hydrothermal spa requirements. Regardless of the size of the project, wet-spa-equipment supplier(s) and consultants should be selected at the outset of the project, so their specific requirements are communicated to the design/construction team.

Common Mistakes

- Delays and re-fits—i.e., additional costs—are usually caused when a wet area specialist is not involved during the preliminary design stages

- Attempting to cut costs by not hiring dedicated specialists, such as MEP consultant or structural engineers; invariably this will cost more money in the long run

- Not specifying properly tested and certified waterproof construction materials

It's important to identify early in the process who is in charge of the coordination of the various sub-contractors. Ideally, this is a project manager who is able to oversee the other contractors and has an understanding of wet area specifications, such as the type of insulation and waterproofing that are necessary; as well as providing insight into the pipe work, sprinkler systems, concrete works, plant rooms, plinths, balance tanks, etc. These will all be installed by various contractors, but the wet area specialist should help get the basics right—such as the floor slab, its water proofing and slope—correct the first time around.

For a large commercial build your wet area team will look like this:
- M&E or MEP consultant: all mechanical and electrical interfaces, including ventilation, plant room, drainage, etc.
- Structural engineer: works on the details of all major building works, including pool structures and prefabricated cabin rooms, etc. (can be part of the architectural team)
- Wet area equipment provider: can work with a wet area design consultant or on own to advise not only on equipment required but also on the layout of cabins, pools and people flow and will ensure plant rooms are properly provided for

International Codes and Standards

Regardless of the country the project is based in, there are internationally accepted codes and standards that hydrothermal specialists follow. In addition to these, you will need to consult your relevant local codes and guidelines. Below is a list of the commonly used codes and standards resources used in professional hydrothermal builds:

International Building Codes: Developed by the International Code Council, a U.S. organization that is dedicated to developing model codes and standards used in the design, build and compliance process to construct safe, sustainable, affordable and resilient structures. These codes are adopted globally; visit www.iccsafe.org

Americans with Disabilities Act (ADA): The disability code adopted by most builders/architects internationally; www.ada.gov

German Sauna Standards: Created by the RAL standards authority; www.ral-guetezeichen.de

Trade Rules of the Swedish Ceramic Tile Council for Wet Areas: Best practices adopted by most hydrothermal experts; www.bkr.se

German DIN 19643-4: German standards for swimming pool water and bath water hygiene; available in English at www.beuth.de

German DIN 18040-1: German barrier-free building standards for disabled acces; www.en.lehnen.de

German DIN 51097: German standards for slip resistance; www.beuth.de

Pool Water Treatment Advisory Group: A UK organization dedicated to raising standards in swimming pool water treatment; www.pwtag.org

BS EN 13451-1:2011, Swimming Pool Safety Requirements: UK standards for general safety and testing of swimming pools and pool equipment; available at shop.bsigroup.com

CIMSPA (Chartered Institute for the Management of Sport and Physical Activity): UK reference guide and training manuals; www.cimspa.co.uk

ÖNORM M6219: Austrian standard for planning and operation of steam baths; www.bdb.at

Chapter Three

Thermal Bathing Areas: Function and Design

· ·

This chapter focuses on thermal bathing cabins and rooms (such as saunas and steam baths) found in a typical modern spa. It includes a comprehensive overview of the functionality and health benefits of the different types of thermal cabins and outlines special considerations required to create spaces that not only please the user, but also comply with accepted health and safety regulations.

· ·

First, we look at some of the guiding principles to follow for ensuring these spaces account for the way people typically interact within them. Design considerations are demanding for the simple reason that users are minimally clothed and are using areas that are both warm and wet, presenting hygiene and safety issues (chapter six).

Human Interaction

When conceiving these areas, it is essential designers understand people fundamentally interact differently when they have few or no clothes on—personal space, in particular, becomes of the utmost importance. The way we interact in a bathing suit or completely naked is very different to how we generally interact in public spaces. Take, for example, public transport—here people often touch strangers, sitting thigh-to-thigh or standing shoulder-to-shoulder on a subway or a bus. By contrast, sitting and touching bare-thigh to bare-

The consideration of personal space is very important when designing thermal bathing areas.

thigh in a sauna or steam room would be unacceptable for most. It seems obvious, but not accounting for the increased need of personal space is one of the biggest mistakes made in a hydrothermal construction project.

In practice this means creating wider hallways in order to avoid any "pinch-points," where people must squeeze past one another; designing benches and seats to allow for adequate space between bodies (600 mm is recommended); and, where possible, providing individual seating so that bathers don't have to consider invading another's personal space on a communal bench.

If you're designing a co-ed (mixed male/female) area, there are other considerations. For example, a standard practice when designing steam rooms and saunas is to include a clear view into the cabin so bathers can see exactly what is happening inside, including gauging the number of current occupants. A woman bathing on her own, for example, may not feel comfortable entering a busy sauna if there are only men inside. She may prefer to wait until some of the group exits or until other women enter the cabin.

Surfaces and Flooring

The surface finishes in all areas of the hydrothermal spa should be chosen based on how well they will accommodate the users. For example, instead of traditional mosaic tile, consider larger slabs of stone or tiling to avoid grout lines every few inches—and to minimize the effects of wear and tear caused by the water's properties. Also, avoid soft, porous stone, such as marble, in steam and wet rooms, as it, too, is prone to degeneration. It's also important to not use very dark tiles so that cleaning staff can easily recognize areas that need cleaning.

The floor finish should be chosen to minimize the potential for slippage. Getting the floor finish and correct sloping angle is crucial for proper drainage, and to avoid accidents in wet areas. In places where a lot of water accumulates, such as those close to pool exits and steam baths, proper drains and slopes need to be implemented in the screed below. Because the drainage in spas is very different to any other part of the building, it needs to be addressed in consultation with the wet-spa-area specialist.

Entries and Exits

Being able to easily enter and exit cabins is paramount. For example, in the event of a bather feeling unwell, he/she should be able to leave the cabin unhindered. This means doors must always open outwards and be free of any mechanical latching devices.

Disabled Access

Access for people with disabilities has become increasingly important in all builds, and the hydrothermal spa area is no exception. Providing this access is not only a law in some countries, but it's also a sign of inclusiveness and enables the facility to market to a broader number of people. And, the benefits of hydrothermal treatments to disabled persons, particularly with motor or physical disabilities, make providing access even more important.

In broad terms, disabled access means incorporating the following basics:
- entry ramps
- correct door widths
- correct clearances on the pull and push side of doors
- low-level bell at the entrance for assisted entry
- a disabled bathroom
- accessible changing and locker rooms, shower areas
- treatment rooms on the ground floor and/or lifts to upper floors
- wheelchair access to treatment rooms (corridors, doors, turning radiuses)
- hydraulic treatment tables

Laws related to disability are enshrined in statutes, such as the Disability Discrimination Act in the UK and the Americans with Disabilities Act in the U.S. These (and others) prohibit discrimination against people with disabilities, which can be visible, hidden, permanent or temporary.

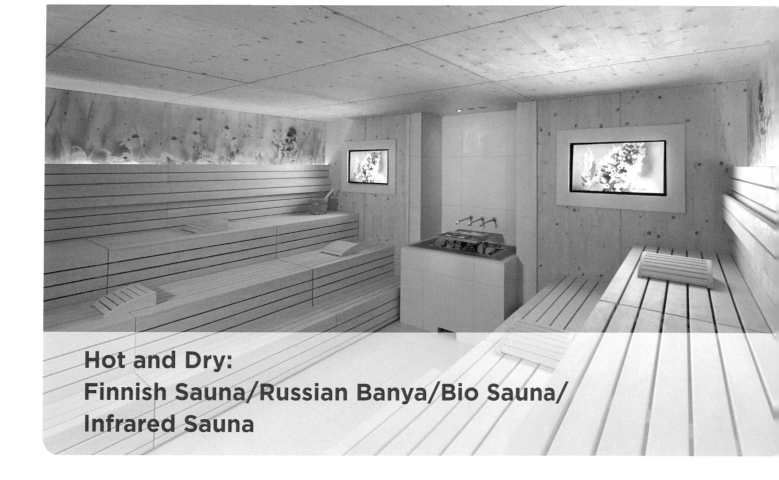

Hot and Dry:
Finnish Sauna/Russian Banya/Bio Sauna/
Infrared Sauna

Finnish Sauna
Temperature: between 80° C to 105° C
Humidity: 5% to 15% at level of second bench; 3% to 10% at level of third bench

Russian Banya
Temperature: between 60° C to 90° C
Humidity: 60% to 70%

Biosauna(or Soft Sauna)
Temperature: between 50° C to 60° C
Humidity: 45% to 65%

Infrared Sauna
Temperature: between 32° C to 35° C
Humidity: 20% to 35%

There are several different styles of saunas in use today. The traditional and most common are Finnish saunas and Russian banyas ("banya" actually means "bathhouse" in Russian, but the term has been adopted to refer to the sauna-like room in the banya). While various sauna types all run at slightly different temperatures and humidity, they are closely related in style, usage and health benefits.

How Saunas Work

A heat source radiates warmth from wood-clad walls via stones that are heated in an electric or gas sauna stove, or, in traditional installations, by log fires.

Saunas typically have two or three different levels of benches to provide room for as many people as possible and also offer varied temperature zones—as the heat will be significantly stronger at higher levels. The benches are wooden and constructed of specialist timber that is chosen for its low thermal conductivity and high laminar strength. The benches have a lattice design with broad slits to allow the air to circulate well throughout the sauna.

Infusions of water bring out an increase in humidity, subjecting the body to a short, but powerful, heat stimulus. Traditionally, a small wooden tub full of water and a ladle was used to pour water over the hot rocks. In addition, the water was often infused with birch twigs to give it a pleasant fragrance—birch was also believed to improve the immune system and open skin pores. In modern installations, automated water dosing systems are often used, and the infusions are typically oil essences in a wide range of scents that offer different aromatherapy stimuli for body and mind.

Type of Use

Saunas are traditionally used to relax and ease muscle tension, as well as boost circulation and improve the immune system.

As one of the hottest therapy cabins in the hydrothermal spa, saunas should be used in conjunction with cold — most traditionally a cold shower, or a "roll in the snow" in the form of a snow cave or igloo. A warm, ankle-deep footbath (outside the sauna cabin) should also be considered for equalizing body temperature. (The small amount of flesh and fat on the feet, combined with a large number of blood vessels, allows them to get cold and hot faster than any other body part, so a footbath will help regulate the body's temperature.)

Health Benefits

The alternation of heat and cold (also called contrast therapy) ensure that a good supply of blood is pumped through the veins, helping to flush out toxins from areas of the body that aren't normally given the ability to do this (namely the skin and subcutaneous tissues). The immersion in both hot and cold is also believed to train the immune system, and regular sauna users rarely suffer minor infections and colds.

Biosauna at Ti Sana, Lombardy, Italy

Heat Source

Sauna Stove: Heat comes from specially sourced stones—typically deep igneous, plutonic rocks capable of absorbing and emitting high levels of heat. They are heated in the sauna stove, traditionally by a wood fire but, more often, by electricity or gas. The size of the sauna stove is determined by how many kilowatts per square meter of heat is required—a calculation that must be done by a wet-area spa specialist. For example, the power requirement of the heater increases if the sauna has any windows or if glass is used within the design in general. If this is the case, there can be a potential health and safety issue for guests.

Doors were traditionally made of wood, but now often feature tempered safety glass.

Materials/Construction

Structure: A soft, sustainable wood that is resin-free is recommended in classic sauna design—common choices are pine, hemlock, spruce and cedar. When choosing wood, note that minimal knots are preferred, as they can act as hot spots and cause uneven heat radiation.

Benches: A hard, low-thermal-conducting wood is required for the benches. Aspen, obeche or poplar are good choices, as they will not split and conduct minimal heat so will avoid burning the skin. Benches should support a minimum of 200 kg/440 lbs per linear meter or 134 lbs per linear foot.

Ceiling: Should not be higher than 226 mm above the head of the bather when sitting on highest bench.

Door: Traditionally made of wood, but design trends have moved towards all glass (must be tempered safety glass). Door sizes can vary depending on application and building codes, particularly in relation to access for the disabled. Interior door handle must be wood so it doesn't become too hot to the touch.

Windows: Though not traditional, windows and/ or glass fronts are becoming more common in modern saunas. Of course, this can change the level of insulation and radiation provided by an all-wood cabin; however, they have architectural and aesthetic merit and can allow bathers to feel more comfortable by delivering more visibility.

Design Considerations

Size/Space: When designing saunas for commercial applications, consideration should be given to personal space and a minimum of 600 millimeters should be allowed for each person sitting. Bathers also like to lie down in a sauna so it should ideally accommodate a two-meter-long person.

Audio/Visual: Consider both lights and sounds to enhance the experience. In commercial builds particularly, audio is used to help break the often-uncomfortable silence you can have when entering a closed space with strangers. There are heat-proof speakers specifically designed for this usage, as well as

- Using the walls of the building when constructing sauna: walls of a sauna must be independent and have a cavity between them and the building walls to avoid condensation

- Installing lighting that is not resistant to the intense heat of a sauna

- Incorrect ventilation that does not provide the correct airflow

- Installing door handles on the inside of the sauna made of material that conducts heat; therefore, scorching bather's hands

- Purchasing a residential sauna for use in a commercial setting—these saunas aren't designed to the same standards

- Using the wrong building materials so that the sauna doesn't function correctly or has a short life span

specialist equipment that links both light and sound output.

Illumination: Lighting choices are fairly limited in saunas simply due to the fact that it has to be resistant to extremely high operating temperatures, especially in the higher section of the sauna, where heat is strongest. There are specifically designed specialty products available for use in saunas, including sconces, crystal glass diffusers and fiber optic lighting. Standard lighting equipment can also be sourced for installation below the first bench level, as heat is less of an issue.

Ventilation: It is essential that saunas are properly ventilated to keep a continual flow of oxygen in the cabin. An air extractor point is located close to the bottom of the cabin to take the cooler, more humid air out, usually via a duct built into the wall panel that will discharge the air at roof level. Fresh air will be delivered directly into the heat source, ideally exchanged and refreshed seven to 10 times per hour.

Special Considerations: Users of the sauna must be able to monitor temperature, relative humidity and the duration of their sauna experience. This makes the inclusion of a thermometer, a hygrometer (used to measure moisture content) and a timer imperative (an 'hour glass' measuring appropriate time segments is ideal).

How to Use a Sauna

- A proper sauna session will take 90 minutes
- Remove clothing, jewelry and contact lenses
- Prior to sauna, users must shower and fully dry themselves to remove any film on the skin that can delay the onset of sweating (ideally, a foot bath should be used)
- Once in the sauna, it's ideal to lie down so that the entire body is within the same temperature zone; if you must sit, sit with your feet up on the same bench you are sitting on
- First sauna session should last eight minutes to 12 minutes (depending on how the body reacts); followed by cooling off 12 minutes to 20 minutes
- Cool off first in the air, then rinse off the sweat with cold water
- The first session can be followed by two more sessions, and you will note that your body will visibly sweat more rapidly during the second and third sessions
- After the final sauna session, it's important to rest and cool off your body completely

How to Use a Banya

- A traditional banya will have a washing room for showering before entering the banya
- Remove clothing, jewelry and contact lenses
- Do a five- to 10-minute session, followed by a cooling-off period either outdoors or in cold water
- During the second session (or "second sweat"), veniks, or bunches of dried branches and leaves from white birch, oak or eucalyptus, may be used to hit bathers (this can be done by yourself or another person) in order to improve circulation
- During the cooling-off period, bathers often sit in an antechamber next to the sauna, socializing, playing games and having refreshments

Infrared Sauna

Temperature: between 32° C to 35° C

Humidity: 20% to 35%

Infrared saunas are the least hot of all the sauna types. The biggest difference is the heat they provide—a natural electromagnetic radiation that's not visible to the human eye. A traditional sauna uses heat to warm the air, which, in turn, warms the body, while an infrared sauna heats the bather's body directly without warming the air. Infrared heat is used in medical applications, as it is believed to enhance blood circulation and ease muscle tension, while strengthening the immune system and reducing stress.

How Infrared Heat Works

Long-wave infrared radiation is absorbed by the upper layers of the skin and is assimilated just under the surface where the heat-sensitive nerves—the peripheral nervous system—are located. This warmth is then distributed throughout the entire body by the blood vessels and lymph nodes and is most comparable to the pleasant warm feeling experienced from the warming of the sun versus the heat provided by UV or X-rays.

Infrared heat is typically delivered via heat storage ceramics; specially designed seats and tiles are available to serve this purpose.

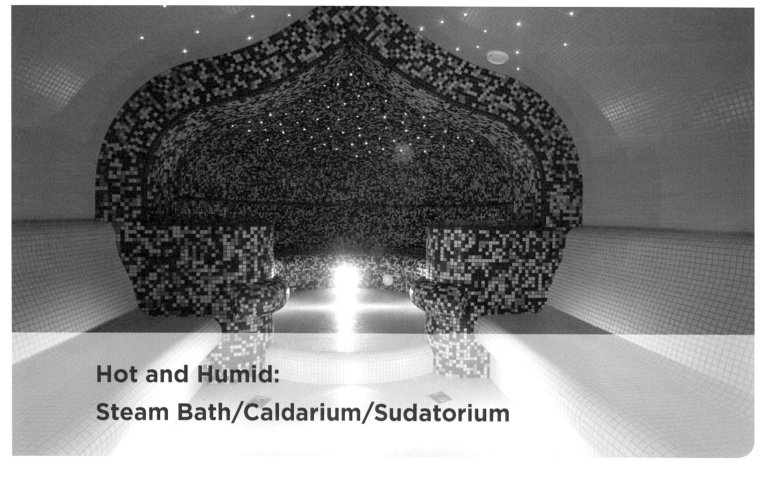

Hot and Humid:
Steam Bath/Caldarium/Sudatorium

**Steam Bath/Caldarium/
Sudatorium**
Temperature: between 40° C to 47° C
Humidity: up to 100%

The caldarium is the Roman precursor to the steam bath (also commonly called steam room). This was the hottest room in the ancient Roman baths—reaching up to 50° C and also had some of the highest humidity rates and air moisture saturation (i.e., steam). This room was heated by an underground furnace known as a "hypocaust," essentially an under-floor heating system that piped hot water throughout the Roman baths. The fire source was typically located just below the caldarium, hence making it the hottest room in the baths, and, above the fire, a pool or cauldron of water resided and acted as the heat source for the room—delivering both heat and steam.

The modern steam bath is unique in that it reaches 100% relative humidity—which gives it the element of steam/fog. It should be noted that in France, a steam bath is called a "hamam"—this can cause some confusion as a traditional Turkish hamam or Moroccan hammam is not equivalent to a steam bath (though smaller, private, hot rooms off the hamam have very similar attributes [see page 31]).

Due to the high moisture, steam baths must be constructed of waterproof materials. One option is foam building boards with reinforced cement coating that will create a waterproof tank, prior to being finished with other water-resistant materials, such as porcelain tile, large custom ceramics, granite, or even acrylic. Thermal insulation provided by foam boards saves not only energy by reducing the working hours of steam generators and the amount of heating required, but it also reduces the maintenance costs of this equipment.

Unlike saunas, steam bath benches are often on a single level because the temperatures are much more consistent throughout the cabin, but a two-tiered bench system can also be used. Continuous surfaces (stone or man-made) are a great choice, but if opting for mosaic, be sure to use grout that is specifically designed to withstand heat and water.

Because of the constant steam, the interior of this room isn't often seen so it's worth considering function over aesthetics when choosing the materials in a steam room.

What makes steam baths so compelling is the damp air they provide—when fine droplets of water come into contact with the air, they provide a negative, energizing charge. Bathers absorb these negatively charged oxygen ions, which can stimulate the metabolism, bringing about increased energy and even claims of fat burning or weight loss. To increase both relaxation and health benefits, aromatherapy is often added to modern steam rooms.

Type of Use

Deep relaxation, detoxification and general wellbeing are key reasons for the enduring popularity of steam baths. Though not as hot as a sauna, steam rooms offer similar benefits at a less intense heat. In traditional Roman baths, this was the hottest area the bathers had access to and, similar to a sauna, should also be used in conjunction with cooling treatments—such as a cold plunge pool (frigidarium), ice room, snow cave or shower.

Health Benefits

The intensive warmth causes the muscles to relax, and limb and joint pain is noticeably reduced. Steam baths are often used to help those that suffer from rheumatism or arthritis. The high humidity also delivers positive moisturizing effects on the skin. As well, the alternation of heat and cold, using a cold plunge pool or snow cave, ensures that a good supply of blood is pumped through the veins, helping to flush out toxins and regulate the blood.

Steam bath at the Swissotel The Bosphorus, Istanbul, Turkey.

Resistive Heat | Electrode

Heat Source

Steam Generator: A steam generator creates steam, which is introduced to the cabin by natural pressure caused by the expansion in the evaporating chamber; the steam travels through an insulated copper pipe and should enter the cabin silently via an open outlet. During the heat-up phase, steam is supplied to the still-cold steam bath, increasing the relative humidity and the temperature. The room climate in a steam room is governed/controlled by the set-point temperature of the room, which is usually 42° C to 47° C. Once that temperature is reached, the steam production is interrupted until the room has cooled down by 2° C to 3° C. When the steam production is off, it is recommended the air extraction fan should be activated. This allows the steam generator to restart steam production quickly and helps keep a constant room humidity of 100%. It also provides visible steam in the room. If the humidity does not reach 95% to 100%, the steam won't be visible.

Steam production is governed by the room's temperature, and a re-ignition of steam is activated when the temperature falls below the desired value, so it's important to be aware that overheating the floors or benches can unbalance the steam generation.

The Principles of Immersion Heating

Heater elements are placed in a closed cylinder and connected to alternating current. The cylinder is filled with tap water, fully demineralized water or partially softened water. Heat generated by the heater elements increases water temperature to approximately 100°C. If fully demineralized water is used, the feed water is practically free of minerals. This ensures long life for the cylinder and heater elements since virtually no mineral deposits can settle or build up, ultimately, this should minimize the number of service/maintenance checks. If tap water is used, some of the minerals that dissolve in the water will settle in the cylinder as solids. These scale deposits are removed by periodic flushing or use of a heavy-duty blow-down pump. The generated steam has a temperature of about 100 °C and minimal positive pressure ("pressure-less" steam). It is also virtually demineralized and germ-free.

Steam generators are housed in a small plant room. These can be designed into the structure or housed separately. It's important to get professional advice on the location and size of your plant room.

The two most common steam bath generators are electrode, which pass electric current through a stainless steel element immersed in water, and resistive heat. Where possible, electrode- or resistive heat-type generators with cleanable and reusable cylinders are recommended. Their integrated drain pumps and flushing systems reduce lime scaling, and this leaves a smaller footprint combined with a more eenvironmentally friendly operation. However, a key contributor to this decision is the type of water available on site, as a resistant-heat steam generator does not rely on water quality and can, therefore, be easily maintained. The water's conductivity depends on its inherent minerals and hardness or softness. Water quality must be tested to determine if an electrode steam generator or a resistive heat-type generator generator should be chosen.

Steam Inlets: The point at which the steam enters the room should be obvious to bathers and in a position that doesn't risk injury from either the hot steam or the nozzle itself. Steam inlets should not be located under benches or allow steam to enter the steam bath under pressure. *Note: Refer to chapter four for more detail on ventilation and climate control.*

Materials/Construction

Structure: One of the most efficient forms of constructing "wet" thermal rooms is using prefabricated, polystyrene panels that are cement-coated and reinforced with fiberglass on both sides. These panels are moisture- and mold-resistant, have high insulating values and are quickly and easily assembled on site. Other materials like acrylic or aluminum/glass can also be used.

Walls/Floors: Made of standard waterproof and mold-resistant materials; floor will have adequate drainage and slope for the water from Kneipp hoses, porcelain tile, granite, large-format, custom ceramics or even man-made surfaces.

Common Mistakes

- Overheating room with floor and wall heating—this will negatively affect humidity/steam

- Installing room temperature sensors in the wrong position, resulting in room not reaching 100% humidity

- Steam outlets dangerously positioned, causing injury to bathers

- Not installing enough correct lighting/illumination; lighting needed to clean the unit is often forgotten

- Failing to install a way to flush/clean benches (a Kneipp Hose, for example)

- Use of wrong materials, such as gypsum boards or plywood, and/or wrong closing mechanisms

- Tiles poorly installed with incorrect grouting—so they easily pop off when exposed to heat and moisture

- Undersizing plant room and/or putting it in the wrong location (i.e., too far away)

- Incorrect ventilation and temperatures

- Using wrong slopes and drainage designs

- Incorrect installation of aroma injection into the steam pipe

- Ceilings too flat with no gradient, causing water to drip on guests

Benches: Ideally continuous stone; can be heated to a surface temperature of 40° C.

Ceiling: Plastered and painted; steam- and etheric oil-resistant plaster; should not be higher than 200 mm above the head of the bather when sitting on highest bench.

Door: Tempered safety glass doors, clear glass to allow for un-obscured viewing. Handles should be stainless

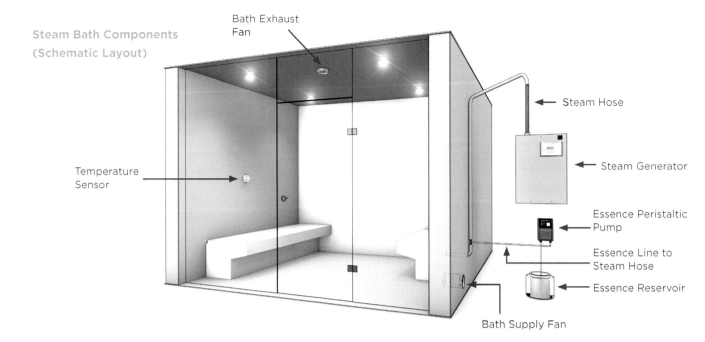

Bath Exhaust Fan

Steam Hose

Steam Generator

Temperature Sensor

Essence Peristaltic Pump

Essence Line to Steam Hose

Essence Reservoir

Bath Supply Fan

steel and doors should push open for easy exit. Doors should be retained, closed by a simple roller-catcher mechanism.

Design Considerations

Size/Space: Bathers like to lie down in a steam bath so it should ideally accommodate a two-meter-long person. When designing steam baths for commercial use, consideration should be given to personal space. The minimum amount you should allow for each person sitting down is 600 millimeters.

Audio/Visual: Steam-proof speakers provided by a specialist wet-area manufacturer can be used. Consider color-changing lighting.

Illumination: Fiber-optic systems offer mood-enhancing illumination, such as star fields or dramatic color changes, and under-bench lighting systems can help with visibility.

Ventilation: Fresh air should be introduced with steam flow; an air outlet in the roof will remove warm air from the steam bath to ensure continuous steam supply and a stable temperature control. Ideally, exhaust ducts should also be installed directly above the exterior of the steam room doors to remove steam that escapes when opening and closing the door.

Special Considerations: Though it's not uncommon to use under-floor and bench heating, be aware that too much heat in the steam room will unsettle the temperature/steam balance.

Mineral deposits from the water can wreak havoc on the steam generator and other components, so look for easy-to-clean systems that seek to minimize these issues, and, instead of relying on tap water, think about using demineralized or soft water.

Consider installing a Kneipp hose for cooling off inside of the cabin. This feature will double as a hygienic way of rinsing benches before and after use.

How to Use a Steam Bath

- Take a shower before entering the steam room—it helps with hygiene, plus, it's best to remove dirt and grime before sweating
- Remove clothing, jewelry and contact lenses
- Up to three sessions inside the steam room is recommended, each one slightly shorter than the previous
- Rest between sessions for 12 minutes to 20 minutes
- When finished let yourself gradually cool down; drink plenty of water
- Clean after use, rinse off space with water; a Kneipp hose is usually provided for this purpose

Warm and Humid:
Turkish Hamam/Moroccan Hammam

Turkish Hamam/Moroccan
(N. African) Hammam
Temperature: between 38° C to 42° C
Humidity: 50% to 80% relative humidity

The Turkish Hamam Experience: Heat (not steam but humidity); followed by a full, vigorous body scrub (with a "kese" or rough mitt); water rinse; a soap massage and rinse; hair wash and rinse. Many modern versions follow that cycle with a full-body oil massage outside of the hamam.

The Moroccan Hammam

Experience: Heat/humidity; followed by a full-body, sticky, black soap massage and exfoliation with a "gome" glove; and then often a terracotta foot stone rub and rinse; a clay/mud application to body, face and hair (and rinse or soak). Also often followed by argan oil application.

The word "hamam" literally translates as "bathroom" in Turkish and refers to the entire Turkish bathhouse. There are two principle styles of hamams—the Turkish hamam and Moroccan or North African hammam. Both derived from the original Roman bathhouses (built after the Romans conquered the respective regions). Upon the Romans' departure, the Turks and North Africans evolved their hamams/hammams to better suit their cultural needs—including the fastidious cleansing of the body (and soul) as a component of the Muslim faith. A strong byproduct of this communal bathing was the socializing element.

A Turkish hamam is a large domed structure with a central room (sikaklek) in which the belly stone (göbek tasi) takes center stage. The belly stone is traditionally where attendants scrub and clean bathers, and there are often small rooms off the large central space that were used for wealthier customers to be washed in private—these design concepts are frequently used in modern hamams for private treatments. There are a large number of basins (called kurnas) around the room that supply water for washing and rinsing,

"Hamam" translates as "bathroom" in Turkish and refers to the entire Turkish bathhouse. Hamams were derived from the original Roman bathhouses.

Common Mistakes

- Confusing a hamam with a steam room—these are different experiences and different room types
- Improper building materials causing issues with cleaning and maintenance
- Forgetting or not providing enough space for plant room
- Poor drainage, causing water to pool on floors
- Not installing temperature and humidity sensors in easily accessed, maintainable conduits
- Placing steam outlet in positions where bathers get injured by the hot steam
- Not installing enough lighting/illumination —often forgotten is the lighting required to clean the unit
- Failing to install a way to flush/clean benches (e.g., a Kneipp hose)

and plenty of bench space where bathers can wait for treatments or relax and socialize.

A Moroccan hammam is similar to its Turkish relation but has retained more of the traditional Roman bathing ritual—sending the bather on a journey through smaller chambers with varying temperatures (like the Roman journey through the laconium, caldarium, frigidarium and tepidarium).

Note that "hamam" is sometimes confusingly used as a generic term to describe a steam bath or a steam room. This is particularly common in France. For clarity, this reference book refers to the hamam as a bathing structure (including communal and treatment areas).

Type of Use

Cleansing was the original purpose of the hamam—and today hygiene still plays a central role. Typical treatments include an exfoliating rub with a "kese" (Turkish) or "gome" (North African) mitten, a soap massage (black soap in North Africa) and hair wash. In addition, socializing and relaxation are the key goals of most bathers.

Health Benefits

The hot air temperature and warmth of the treatment surface (whether a traditional belly stone or a modern heated treatment table) relieve muscle pain and promote mental relaxation, while the high humidity produces intense sweating, which leads to a detoxifying cleansing.

Heat Source

Traditionally, a hypocaust provided warm under-floor heating, replaced by hot water "hydronic" systems as piped plumbing systems were developed. Often the floors were heated higher than body temperature, requiring bathers to wear wooden sandals (which became serious fashion statements in the heyday of Turkish hamams). A modern hamam will use hydronic heating, a system of pipes heating the floor, walls and benches to maintain a high radiated temperature.

Unlike a steam bath, the hamam does not operate at close to 100% humidity. A high level of humidity (50% to 80%) is required, however, and this was traditionally generated by the large amount of water being used in the treatments and evaporating off the hot floors and seating/treatment surfaces. Today's guests aren't always comfortable with the public bathing rituals so massage, exfoliation, shaving and hair washing may be undertaken in private rooms. This means humidity levels often need to be augmented in other ways—either through a steam generator or water-misting system with appropriate venting and air circulation systems.

These are connected to humidity and temperature sensors, allowing for accurate control of the hamam environment.

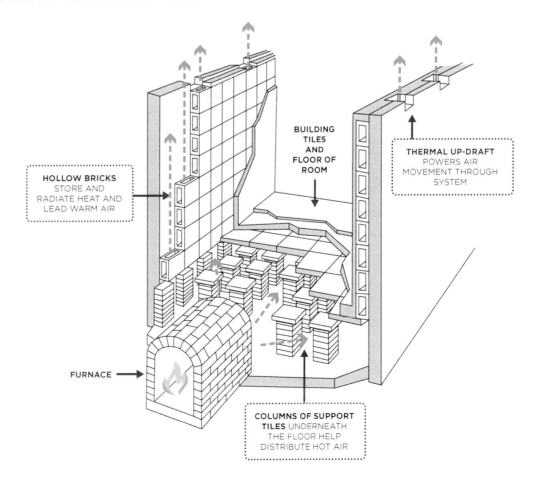

In ancient Roman bathhouses, a hypocaust system was used to heat the rooms—similar to today's hydronic systems.

HOLLOW BRICKS STORE AND RADIATE HEAT AND LEAD WARM AIR

BUILDING TILES AND FLOOR OF ROOM

THERMAL UP-DRAFT POWERS AIR MOVEMENT THROUGH SYSTEM

FURNACE

COLUMNS OF SUPPORT TILES UNDERNEATH THE FLOOR HELP DISTRIBUTE HOT AIR

Materials/Construction

Structure: One of the most efficient forms of constructing "wet" thermal rooms is using prefabricated, polystyrene panels that are cement-coated and reinforced with fiberglass on both sides. These panels are moisture- and mold-resistant, have high insulating values and are quickly and easily assembled on site.

Walls: Porcelain tile, marble, granite, or even man-made surfaces like Avonite, Silestone and other agglomerates

Floors: Prefabricated tileable floors with integrated gradient and warrantied waterproofing. Stone tiling with integral drains set into the floor to avoid pooling of water and to aid cleaning and maintenance. Slip-resistant surfaces are essential (following the German DIN 5109-7 standards for barefoot traffic, classification B, is ideal).

Benches/Göbek Tasi: Finished using continuous stone surfaces (or similar man-made surfaces); if opting for a special pattern or design, use grout that is resistant to water and heat.. Note the göbek tasi is often still present, usually as an acknowledgment to tradition rather than a dedicated treatment surface, but keeping this traditional "amphitheatre" style is popular and provides a large surface for lying down.

Ceiling: Plastered and painted, ssteam- and etheric oil-resistant plaster. May be tiled/include ornamentation for aesthetic considerations

Lighting: Traditional hamams have piercings in the domed roof, sometimes in quite intricate shapes, allowing sunlight to shaft through these "elephant eyes," which often have diameters of 10 cm to 15 cm. Modern lighting technology can be used to replicate these ideas, from simple, round downlights to complex systems where lighting projectors shine through to replicate the shafts of sunlight in traditional settings.

Hamam at the Swissotel The Bosphorus, Istanbul, Turkey.

In a traditional hamam, there are a large number of basins (called kurnas) around the room for washing and rinsing, and plenty of bench space where bathers can wait for treatments or relax and socialize.

Design Considerations

Size/Space: The ceiling should be designed to include a traditional domed cupola roof or vaulted ceiling. It may be appropriate for heat recovery systems to be installed to re-circulate the heat at higher levels.

Aromatherapy: automatic essential oil dosing system

Audio/Visual: Low-level audio with water/steam proof speakers

Illumination: soft, indirect lighting from LED and fiber optic

Ventilation: Fresh air supply and air extraction to ensure good oxygen levels

Special Considerations: An authentic atmosphere is achieved when the room is finished in traditional Turkish "Iznik"-style tiles and Carrara Blanco marble; while orth African hammams favor a traditional plaster finish called "tadelakt," which isn't advised in commercial applications. Although there are some excellent modern plasters that can achieve the same effect, dramatic designs have been created in modern hamams using-less traditional species of natural stone and tile.

How to Use a Traditional Hamam/Hammam

- Take a shower before entering hamam/hammam

- In a public bath, you will be given a "pestamal" (a towel with fringed ends)

- Enter the dry, warm room to start the bathing process

- When moving to the hot room, women usually remove their towels, while men traditionally keep theirs on. Women and men bathe separately.

- Use the basins ("kurnas") to cool down with cool water while in the hot room

- Await cleansing rituals, including exfoliation, hair washing, shaving, etc.

- This can be followed by a private massage

Warm and Dry:
Laconium; Tepidarium/Warm Relaxation Room

Laconium
Temperature: between 38° C to 45° C
Humidity: between 10% to 20%

Tepidarium/Warm
Relaxation Room
Temperature: between 30° C to 40° C
Humidity: between 20% to 40%
(not controlled)

Laconium

The laconium is a relaxing, dry heat environment with a temperature below the aggressive levels of a Finnish sauna. In Roman times, it was seen as the dry, sweating room of the thermae, adjacent to the caldarium steam room with its higher temperature. It provides a more relaxing, less-intense experience allowing for a longer treatment—usually 20 minutes but up to an hour. It is recommended for individuals that find the dry 80° C to 105° C heat of the sauna too hot and the 100% humidity of the steam room too high.

The laconium plays an important role in many spas for guests who have contra-indications (such as pregnancy or cardiovascular conditions) that prevent them from using the hotter rooms. Offering this option makes the spa more inclusive.

Type of Use

At a temperature of 38° C to 45° C and relatively low humidity, the laconium environment is relaxing. Sitting or lying on warm/hot benches and loungers warms the body quickly and helps start the sweating process. Cold-water Kneipp hoses are available to wash away perspiration, creating a hot-cold purification and detoxification cycle.

Health Benefits

The purpose of the laconium is to purify and detoxify the body by stimulating circulation. The heat-based treatment improves blood flow, increases metabolism, promotes mental and physical relaxation and reduces stress. Applying essential oils such as lavender, eucalyptus and citrus to the skin can also enhance the positive effects of the heat—promoting mind-and-body re-generation. Aromatherapy oils are often used in the laconium for the same purpose.

Heat Source

The heat is radiated evenly from the walls, floor and reclining surfaces. In Roman times, this was provided by under-floor hot air in the hypocaust. In modern times, the dry heat is generated by electrical elements or piped hydronic hot water systems within the walls, floors and benches themselves. The surface temperature of the seats is around 30° C to 35° C, the floors 40° C to 45° C and the walls 60° C to 70° C.

Materials/Construction

Structure: Generally ample in size, with enough room to seat six to 16 people. The interior is usually tiled to provide both the radiated heat surface and a pleasing aesthetic.

Walls/Floors: Made of standard waterproof and mold-resistant materials; floor will have adequate drainage and slope for the water from Kneipp hoses. Prefabricated, tileable shower bases with integrated gradient and sealing are an option.

Benches: Ideally continuous stone or other waterproof material to minimize/avoid grouting. Almost always static and fixed to the floor to allow for heating element to be connected; temperature is between 30° C to 35° C.

Ceilings: Can be tiled for effect, but, otherwise, coated in waterproof paint.

Door: A self-closing door is required to retain the heat in the room.

Heated, body form loungers are ideal in relaxation rooms.

Design Considerations

Walls/Benches/Floors: As the laconium is a steam-free environment that bathers remain in for extended periods of time; the interior usually reflects a luxury environment and is often opulent in its tiling and fittings.

Audio/Visual: Low-level and ceiling lighting, together with discreet music, can enhance the relaxing atmosphere. Placement of equipment requires careful consideration; equipment must be accessible for maintenance.

Special Considerations: The room needs regular cleaning to ensure acceptable hygiene standards so drainage system should take this into account. Guests may be using this space to relax after the intense heat of a steam room or sauna so chilled refreshments are often offered in this space, even if it is only a chilled water fountain.

How to Use the Laconium

- The laconium can be a specific heat-based relaxation treatment, and it can also be part of a spa cycle preparing the body for more extreme temperatures

- Wear a towel to protect the skin from the hot reclining surfaces, as well as for hygienic reasons

- Sit or lay for periods long enough to allow perspiration from the body

- Use Kneipp hoses to wash off sweat and encourage blood circulation, particularly to the extremities

- Repeat the cycle

Tepidarium/Warm Relaxation Room

In ancient Roman baths, the tepidarium had a central role as a relaxation and body care room. Typically the air temperature would be warm (tepidus), around 30° C to 40° C with constant radiant heat, at a higher temperature, coming from the stone walls, floors, bench seating and individual recliners.

The tepidarium was often the central hub of a Roman bath, linked to other hot and cold rooms. Bathers would use the tepidarium as a focal point for warming up the body, engaging in body treatments (oils and cleaning), as well as relaxation. In a modern spa, this area is usually referred to as the "relaxation room" and will often have individual stone/tile recliners and bench seating with thermostatically controlled electric or hydronic heating. Of course, many "relaxation rooms" today feature normal beds or cushioned loungers, but they often have an element of warmth to them and their concept has derived from the traditional tepidarium.

Type of Use

The tepidarium is traditionally used to warm up the body before using other baths, as well as to recharge body energy through heat from the floor, walls and fixtures. It can, of course, be used for gently cooling down following periods in a sauna or steam bath, or indeed warming up after using a plunge pool, cold shower, ice room or snow room. It provides a counterpart to other hot and cold treatments and is also a key relaxation area in the modern spa.

Health Benefits

The radiant heat offers deep tissue/muscle penetration to soothe and relax individuals.

Heat Source

In a modern spa, air temperature is controlled by the central heating system (warm air ducts) with electric or hydronic under-floor heating. An under-floor heating system adds considerable flexibility to the heat source, and, although initially more expensive to install, has cost efficiencies over a longer term.

An alternative to heated, body forming loungers are soft, warm beds—water beds offer a nice alternative to traditional mattresses.

- Room lacks the privacy guests desire or is not big enough or too bright for relaxation

- Choice of loungers uncomfortable—too small or too hard

- Use of incorrect building materials

- Allowing noise from plant rooms or other treatment rooms to infiltrate relaxation area

- Incorrect ventilation and temperature

- Aromatherapy is often overlooked

Benches and recliners have additional hydronic or electrical heating to increase the radiated heat/infrared heat level. The benches and recliners are often fixed (non-moveable) fittings.

Materials/Construction

Structure: Generally ample in size, with enough room to seat six to 16 people. The interior is usually tiled to provide both the radiated heat surface and a pleasing aesthetic.

Walls/Floor: Usually of ceramic tile/stone to maximize the radiated heat, and, like the laconium, are often more ornate because they are dry, and bathers spend a great deal of time in them.

Benches/Loungers: Also of stone and tile for the same radiated-heat benefit. Loungers are contoured to allow for comfortable relaxation with individual thermostats to control radiated-heat temperature. Loungers are often two-piece—a base pedestal and a horizontal reclining surface, often tiled with mosaic to enhance the aesthetic appeal of the room. Other surfaces include stone and ceramic, which minimize joints—improving comfort and facilitating cleaning.

Ceilings: Can be tiled for effect, but, otherwise, coated in waterproof paint.

Door: A self-closing door is required to retain the heat in the room.

Design Considerations

Size/Space: The overall size is generally dependent on the other bathing facilities/overall capacity of the spa. Individual loungers need to encourage relaxation usage and should be approximately 700 mm x 1,800 mm x 900 mm (w x l x h).

Audio/Visual: Low-level and ceiling lighting, together with discreet music, can enhance the relaxing atmosphere. Care needs to taken with placement of equipment which needs to be accessible for maintenance Tepidarium does not have extreme heat/cold or specific water applications so the construction does not necessarily have to be as robust as other bathing areas.

Surfaces and fittings should be waterproof, however and electrical elements must be sealed and protected (with circuit protection/circuit breaker capability) to allow for cleaning and maintenance. As the Tepidarium is a relaxation area, a key focus is the design aesthetics, including audio and lighting. The provision of privacy areas using screens and curtains is common.

How to Use a Tepidarium

- Use this area to acclimatize to higher temperatures prior to using other bathing rooms

- Always use a towel to recline on

- Relax in the room, following hot/cold and water/dry treatments

- Use individual audio/other sensory facilities (if provided) to enhance relaxation and feeling of wellbeing

Cold:
Plunge Pool/Frigidarium; Ice Cave;
Igloo; Snow Rooms

Plunge Pool/Frigidarium
Temperature: between 5° C to 20° C
Humidity: Not controlled

Ice Cave/Igloo
Temperature: between 7° C to 15° C
Humidity: Not controlled

Snow Rooms
Temperature: below 0° C
Humidity: Not controlled

The traditional frigidarium is a large cold-water pool, typically entered after the hot caldarium (steam bath), warm laconium and tepidarium (relaxation). It was considered a key part of the thermae journey and served to cool down bathers between hot treatments (akin to the Finnish "roll in the snow" after the sauna), as well as close the pores of the skin after exposure to heat before leaving the baths. The cold water traditionally came from mountain streams, cold springs or underground cisterns.

Just as the Roman baths had variations on the frigidarium, including plunge baths, cold-water pours and cold swimming pools, so the modern interpretation includes snow and ice treatments to maximize the "chill" concept.

Type of Use

The frigidarium can be a starting point in a spa bathing experience, or, more commonly, used as a cool-down element within the spa bathing cycle. The availability of modern refrigeration technology has allowed for much innovation, and cold pools are often supplemented

Cold experiences are designed to recreate the feeling of stepping out into a snowy landscape or jumping into a cold body of water.

by ice bowls and fountains, "shock" showers, cool-air blasts and snow caves/cabins. These can be individually placed near the warmer cabins, providing "on-demand" cooling, as well as mandatory elements of a heating/cooling spa cycle.

Health Benefits

After exposure to a hot environment (sauna/steam bath), the body typically experiences a physiological slowdown, entering a semi-inertia state. The surface capillaries of the skin are dilated, blood pressure is lowered, the skin has a high color and there is a general deprivation of blood to internal organs. These conditions, plus external sweating, persist while the body cools down. The cool temperature of the frigidarium speeds up the cool-down process and accelerates this when cold water and snow/ice are applied.

Similar to the sauna/banya heat and cold contrast therapy, the cooling-down process accelerates the supply of blood to the skin and internal organs, facilitates toxin flush out and closes the skin pores to prevent dehydration.

The vascular dilation provided by the heat and rapid contraction from the cold enables the slowed-down, cooled blood to act as a "pipe cleaner" for the restricting fine-membrane arteries.

Cold rooms, such as ice caves, igloos and snow rooms, have an additional benefit: because the atmosphere is also near-freezing temperatures, cold air can be breathed deeply into the lungs. This delivers the benefit of vascular dilation in the lungs, an area that is very difficult to reach through the epidermal or surface shock that cold pools or showers provide. In colder climates, during evenings and autumn/winter, this cold-air benefit can also be provided with access to outside spaces.

Cold Source

The frigidarium pool commonly uses standard cold water, but this must be filtered and treated the same way as any public bathing pool and chillers. Heat exchangers are also used to maintain temperatures (in busy spas, the water will soon warm up from frequent use). Applications of ice and snow require placement of ice-/snow-making machines—snow can only be provided in a specially designed room with specialist equipment, while ice fountains can take up little space and use localized, flaked, ice machines specially designed and adapted to deliver ice either on demand or to a level-controlled, decorative vessel.

Materials/Construction

Structure: One of the most efficient forms of constructing "wet" thermal rooms is using prefabricated, polystyrene panels that are cement-coated and reinforced with fiberglass on both sides. These panels are moisture- and mold-resistant, have high insulating values and are quickly and easily assembled on site. Another option for cold rooms are 10-cm metal sandwich plates, powder-coated outside.

Common Mistakes

- Using incorrect building materials; lacking the insulation needed to keep room cool
- Cooling with too much air flow or incorrect cooling systems
- Plunge pools often designed with ineffective ways to enter and exit—stairs too high or no railing

Walls/Floors: In general, these reflect the overall design requirements and are usually tiled in mosaic or other small-format tiling. Floors should have adequate drainage to reflect high water usage and radiant under-floor heating to facilitate cleaning and maintenance.

Benches: Not required in this "cool down" facility because there is no relaxation component.

Ceiling: Textured/non-drip render complemented by design requirements (tile, etc.).

Ice Fountains take up very little space and use flaked ice machines that deliver ice either on demand or in controlled amounts to a decorative vessel.

Design Considerations

Size/Space: The frigidarium concept is flexible (however, minimum-depth rules must be observed) in that it can include everything from cold-water swimming pools to small-diameter plunge pools. A common alternative is the chilled-water "shock" shower with 25-second to 75-second timers.

Ventilation: Re-circulating chilled air can facilitate the temperature requirement, and cold-air "blasts" can be used as specific treatment stations.

Special Considerations: It can be helpful to physically separate the hot and cold areas of the spa to maximize energy efficiency and minimize construction complexity. Individual ice/shower stations should be incorporated in the overall design—a strong cooling process in the immediate vicinity of high-temperature facilities is both physically restorative and appreciated by users.

Also, whenever a plunge pool is featured, a shower should be nearby for bathers to rinse off before entering—this will vastly improve the cleanliness of the pool water, reducing pressure on the filtration system and ultimately reducing water loss through less-frequent need for backwashing the filters.

How to Use a Frigidarium

- Immediately follow a high-temperature treatment with a cool-down process

- Use individual treatment stations, such as ice fountains and air nozzles, to maximize the recirculation "tingle"

- Use cold showers, cold pools and cold plunge pools as more-invasive cooling treatments.

- Move on to the next part of the process—additional heat cycles or relaxation therapy

- Always allow body temperatures to fully normalize before using another hot experience; this can take 15 minutes to 20 minutes for most people, as the surface cooling from water, ice or snow, will take far longer to reach the core of the body

Ice caves, igloos and snow rooms provide a cold contrast to the heat therapies in a hydrothermal spa.

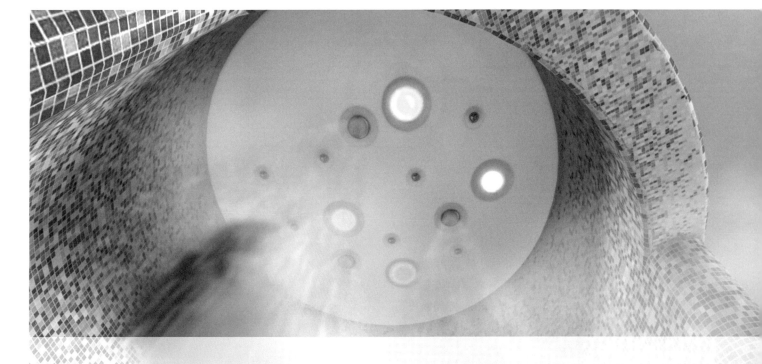

Warm/Cold and Wet:
Experience Showers

Warm and cold waters have always been integral to the thermal bathing ritual—allowing the body to cool down—and are key elements of the traditional tepidarium and frigidarium. A more modern interpretation is using a standard shower for a quick cool down after a sauna or steam bath.

In recent years, this has evolved into the "experience shower"—a combination of water, sound and smell that evokes a natural "event" for the bather, with themes ranging from "emotional showers" and "energy showers" to "waterfall/deluge showers" and "monsoon showers" to many in between.

Type of Use

An essential part of thermal bathing is cooling the body down—this is important for enjoying spa facilities safely and maximizing health benefits. The experience shower goes further than a simple shower by adding an entertainment element to the everyday activity of showering.

Typically, the experience shower combines water flow variations, sounds and music, dynamic lighting and even aromatherapy to deliver a multi-sensory stimulus.

The key element in the showers is the water jets that can be programmed to deliver different experiences. Strong, lateral jets facilitate massage, overhead water buckets deliver a dump of cold water, and water mists gently hydrate, while temperature-contrast showers deliver water. Jets can also be programmed to mimic nature; for instance, rain, thunderstorm, mist and waterfall. A handheld showerhead is often included for washing prior to a sauna or steam treatment, as well as for providing additional cooling.

Some common Experience Shower themes include Rain Forest, Tropical Rain, Cold Waterfall, Polar Mist, Monsoon, Summer Storm, etc. An individual shower enclosure often has several pre-programmed themes that last between 30 seconds to three minutes.

Health Benefits

Body cooling after heat treatments ensures a good supply of blood to the skin and internal organs, helps to flush out toxins and closes skin pores. The multi-sensory experience-shower approach also adds stimulation of the senses—driving other emotional responses, ranging from excitement to contentment. This offers a unique, new element to the overall wellness benefits.

Heat/Cold Source

Hot and cold water are piped to the showerheads. Sufficient water pressure/capacity is essential to maintain the multi-head shower flows.

Materials/Construction

Structure: Size and shape (square, round, snail, etc.) depends on the site layout. Specially designed, prefabricated, polystyrene panels that are cement-coated and reinforced with fiberglass on both sides, should be moisture-resistant and waterproof.

Walls/Floors: Usually tiled; drainage capacity/floor slope is a key element of a successful design. Prefabricated, tileable shower bases with integrated gradient and sealing are a good option.

Experience showers combine water, sound and smell to evoke a natural "event" for a bather.

Design Considerations

Size/Space: Enclosures are typically for a single person. Size is approximately 140 cm x 140 cm x 250 cm if square and 120 cm in diameter if round. However, a rule of thumb is to never create a shower smaller than 100 cm x 100 cm x 250 cm or larger than 200 cm x 200 cm x 250 cm. Height can vary between 220 cm to 300 cm.

Audio/Visual: Music and sounds are generated by an integrated MP3 player with memory card and activated through the control panel. Common sounds include tropical rain, thunder, waterfall, birdsong, waves/sea, river/stream, etc. A water-resistant, mounted speaker(s) on the ceiling offers the audio. LED lighting provides visual cues to support the experience—dark skies, sunset, sunrise, etc., and smells like fruit, flowers, spices, and sea, can be added to enhance the experience.

⚠ Common Mistakes

- Not having enough water pressure to make shower experience operate correctly
- Water quality—hard or dirty water will ruin equipment and create a bad guest experience
- Improper sealing of electrical and hydraulic equipment within shower
- Incorrect calculation of draining slope and draining capacity
- Shower cabinets can be too big, causing an unpleasant shower experience
- Plant room forgotten or too far from showers
- Overuse of aromas

Experience-shower controller showing three different experiences: tropical rain, cold mist, Caribbean storm.

Aromatherapy: A dosing system linked to the control panel provides the fragrance. This level of technology requires adequate space for placement and easy access for maintenance, as well as robust waterproofing. In addition, it's imperative to ensure that the aroma does not flow back into the local water supply.

Special Considerations: Positioning is usually in proximity to heat treatment rooms. Additional features, such as simulated wind/breeze, can also be added, requiring additional ventilation.

An experience shower consists of a lot of components in a relatively small structure, so placement, access and waterproofing are key aspects of a successful installation—as is the overall management of water quality, pressure and drainage.

In order to cut corners or save money, some facilities opt for a "standard" shower, but standing under a cool/cold shower for 30 seconds to 180 seconds, the ideal time required to start the cooling process, can be very uninspiring. The features offered by Experience Showers are designed to hold the bather's interest and act as a distraction; consequently, there is a greater chance of the bather getting the full cooling treatment and deriving maximum benefit.

How to Use an Experience Shower

- Pre-programmed experiences are selected from a push-button control panel

- The user stands in the water jet area as the program runs

- Different programs can be experienced

- Handheld showers/Kneipp hoses can be used for individual cleaning/cooling requirements

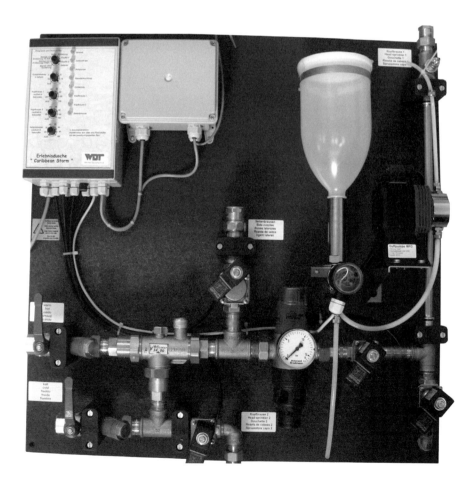

The controller, dosing pump and other equipment used to run an experience shower.

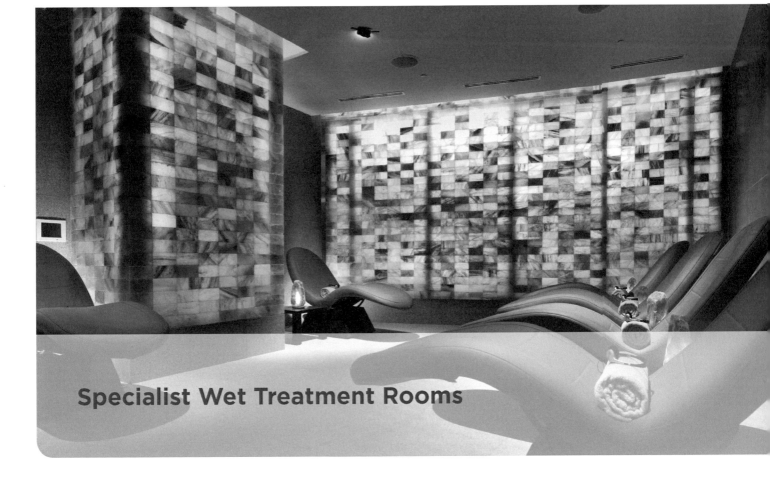

Specialist Wet Treatment Rooms

Inhalation Rooms
Steam with Essential Oils
Oxygen
Salt

Mud Bath Rooms

Vichy Shower

Hydrotherapy Tub

Floatation Tank

Dry Floatation Bed

In addition to the communal-based hydrothermal areas, individual rooms are often used for specific treatments or therapies. Many of these combine the structural and thermal elements of the main rooms but are generally smaller in size.

Inhalation Rooms

Although aromatherapy essential oils are often present in other rooms, an inhalation room delivers a more specific treatment for the use of inhaled agents to treat respiratory conditions. The goal of inhalation therapy (also called respiratory therapy) is to improve respiration and can be a specific treatment for chronic conditions such as asthma, bronchitis and emphysema.

Steam with Essential Oils

Typically, an inhalation room will focus on steam inhalation combined with essential oils that target the upper respiratory tract, nose and sinuses. A variety of essential oils can be used (individually or combined), such as cedarwood, eucalyptus, pine, sandalwood, rosemary, tea tree and frankincense. The structure of the room will be similar to a steam room—medium-hot with a high humidity—with ergonomic benches, a low-volume steam generator, ventilation and an essential oil infuser or automatic dosing system, in which the essence of essential oils is infused into the flow of steam that enters the room.

Oxygen

Oxygen therapy increases the oxygen level in the bloodstream and is usually administered through a tube or mask at a specific inhalation station, or as part of an integral system built into a sauna, where guests are able to directly inhale oxygen via dedicated dispenser hoses.

Salt

Salt therapy originated in Europe with natural salt caves and caverns—it is alleged that workers in salt mines had a significantly reduced number of respiratory issues than other mine workers. Claimed to relieve asthma, improve circulation and lower blood pressure, salt rooms and caves are specific treatment rooms requiring dry conditions, good ventilation and copious amounts of salt on the floor, walls and ceiling. Many believe the only way to truly benefit from salt inhalation is through the introduction of finely powdered salt into the air or by nebulizing brine

vapor into the space. The treatment is passive—the individual sits in a comfortable recliner, often with a blanket and mood music/lights to enhance the state of relaxation.

Mud Bath Rooms

Mud bathing originated thousands of years ago as a medicinal and beautifying ritual—depending on the minerals inherent in the mud, they can cleanse, exfoliate, absorb toxins, increase circulation and soften the skin.

The mud treatment ritual typically takes place in a specially designed area, and either a therapist is on hand to apply the mud, or bathers will apply it to one another. After taking a shower, various types of mud are applied to different parts of the body. Then bathers enter a warm, herb-infused steam bath to encourage relaxation and detoxification. The mud needs to be kept moist so the correct degree of humidity must be maintained. After 20 minutes or so, an automatic "rain" system showers the room, starting the process of removing the mud. This is usually augmented by additional showering, followed by the application of moisturizer to the body.

Inhalation rooms combine steam with essential oils that target the upper respiratory tract, nose and sinuses using essential oils such as cedarwood, eucalyptus, pine, sandalwood, rosemary, tea tree and frankincense.

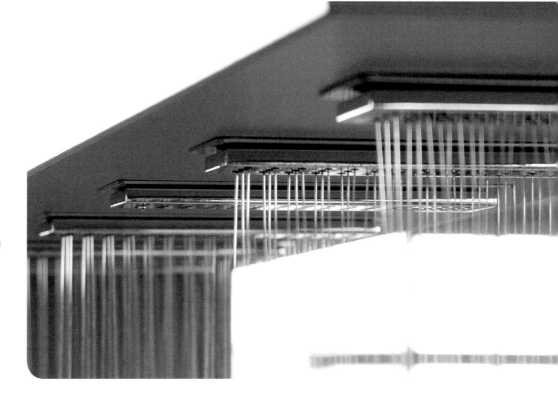

A contemporary Vichy shower design showing a series of shower bars that are used to keep clients warm, hydrate the skin and soothe/relax muscles.

In addition to the above mud bath ritual, there is also the practice of immersing fully in mud or being wrapped in mud to soak up its positive effects.

A specialized mud bath room needs to incorporate showering facilities, steam and heating elements, relaxation benches/recliners and adequate drainage. The design will normally consist of two rooms: the actual mud bathing chamber and an ante room where guests can disrobe, shower post-treatment and, space permitting, receive the warm, oil moisturizing massage to complete the experience.

Vichy Shower

The term Vichy shower originates from the thermal spa of Vichy in France. Originally, a Vichy shower was a manual massage by two therapists while taking the shower.

Now, the standard treatment is carried out by one therapist whose work is made easier by modern Vichy showers that allow for easy and quick adjustability of the shower heads.

The relaxing effect of the warm water on the muscles make the body more receptive to the massage. The main benefits of the shower itself are increased blood circulation caused by the flow of the water, a hydration of the body that fights off fatigue and prevents acne,

and a reduction of stress and toxins by stimulating the nerve response in the skin.

Further benefits result from massage oils or other products being used during the treatment, adding to the positive properties of the Vichy shower. Similarly, the type of water being used, e.g. thermal or mineral water, changes the effects of the treatment.

A Vichy shower is a horizontal series of showerheads forming a "rain bar" over a waterproof, cushioned table that features drainage on the side for all the excess water. The therapist gives a manual massage, and the water is used to keep the customer warm, to hydrate the skin and soothe/relax muscles. Vichy treatments are often combined with other treatments, such as massages, using specific products and/or body wraps or other, classical wet table treatments.

The Vichy shower and wet massage table is usually a permanent, bespoke piece of equipment that requires hot/cold water supply and drainage and adequate space for both the table and therapist—typically, a table will be 1.0 m x 2.5 m and will require a minimum of 800 mm of working room around the sides of the table. The rain-bar component is usually designed to swivel away from the table to allow for an unobstructed entry and exit on the table, in addition to creating space so that the room and table can be used for other treatments.

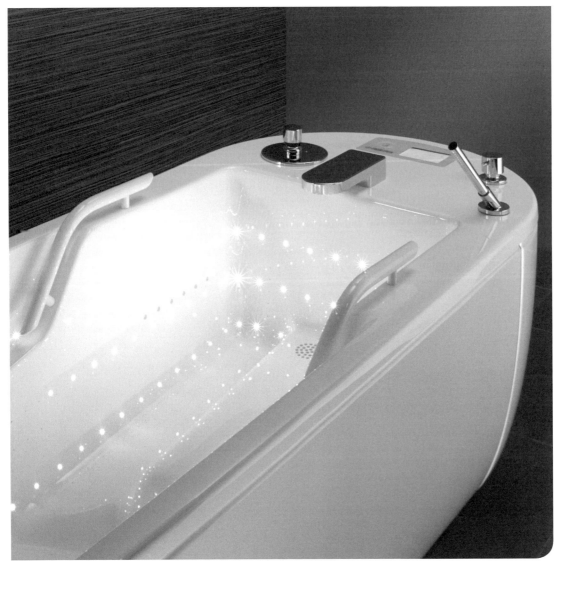

Today's hydrotherapy tubs offer sequential massage, starting with the feet and moving up the body.

Hydrotherapy Tub

An important part of the underwater-pressure-jet massage is the relaxation of the muscular system inside the warm water. This enables the massage jets to deeply penetrate the muscles.

Modern units offer a sequential massage, starting with the feet and going towards the upper part of the body in small steps. In addition, the massage pressure can be regulated automatically. The intensity of the massage can thus be reduced both in the beginning and the end of the treatment.

Individual hydrotherapy tubs deliver a unique sensation of heat, buoyancy and hydro-massage. Often used without the aid of a therapist, the jets are positioned to stimulate and relax trigger points in the body. Aromatherapy oil can be added to the baths to intensify the bather's relaxation and engage the other senses; soothing skin products are also often featured. The natural healing power of mineral water or seawater can increase the effectiveness of the treatment. In addition, therapist-assisted treatments can be performed, which allow for the combination of both physical touch and hydro-massage.

Floatation Tank

Floatation (sometimes spelled "flotation") tanks are also known as isolation or sensory-deprivation tanks. These are self-contained, enclosed units filled with less than 30 cm of salt water that are said to rejuvenate users by putting them into a meditative state. The buoyancy of the salt also frees the body from tension, increases blood circulation and removes all pressure from joints.

Dry Floatation Bed

Treatments on dry floatation beds are often carried out in combination with a body wrap. The bather lies on a membrane suspended within a tank filled with warm water that gives a sensation of weightlessness. Some beds include jets underneath the waterproof covering to provide a gentle hydro-massage.

Due to their stable lying surface, some units can also be used for manual massages. A multitude of different treatments can thus be performed inside one room using the same unit.

The units are often height-adjustable, which allows for more ergonomic working conditions for the therapist.

In addition to the relaxing effect of "floating," the benefits of dry float depend on the products being used. Cosmetic, dermatologic or therapeutic packs are applied. The warmth of the water supports the effect of the packs, making their absorption into the skin much easier. An additional benefit is the feeling of sinking into and lying in, or rather on, a surface of water.

Body Wraps

Often body wraps are paired with dry floatation treatments. Body wraps can be partial (treating only parts of the body) or full body.

Varying products and media are used in body wraps, and the benefits correlate directly to the components present in the media. Traditionally, wraps were predominantly mineral-based (sludge, mud, peat, moor) and, today, many treatments still use similar organic materials. In addition, wraps are now often complemented with cosmetic, dermatologic or other products.

A few examples of the wellbeing benefits:
- Detoxification (peloids and algae)
- Revitalization (cosmetic wraps, peloids, algae)
- Slimming (algae)
- Reduction of cellulite (algae)
- Moisturizing of the skin (cosmetic products)

Not only does the heat used in these treatments encourage the absorption of the media by the body, but it also helps promote relaxation, relieve stress and even work to increase blood circulation.

Body wraps are often applied on a standard therapeutic table, however, dry floatation systems can offer a better experience. The dry floatation bed will have a solid surface in the beginning, making it easier for the customer to lie down and enable the application of the body wrap. After, the guest sinks into a cushion of warm water and experiences a "floating" feeling. The warm temperature of the water supports the effect of the body wrap. When the treatment is coming to an end, the surface of the bed will become solid again, and the guest will be moved up, out of the water cushion, making it easier to exit the bed.

Treatment Room Equipment

The installation of other water equipment is common to add versatility to treatment rooms:

- Scotch hose: Providing alternating hot and cold water (at many different temperatures) under pressure to 'jet blitz' the standing bather. The combination of heat, cold and pressure stimulates blood and lymph circulation and massages the major muscle groups.

- Kneipp hose: A freestanding low-pressure hose/shower head used for cooling down in the team room or communal shower area. Also popular in rooms used for mud treatments to help with washing off the mud applications.

- Dosing pumps: Adding essence of essential oils to the water flow to enhance the aromatherapy and physical experiences.

Treatment Room Design

The rooms where these treatments take place have their own set of requirements.

All modern wet treatment rooms should have space for a shower within the room, ideally in an anteroom so the guest can shower in private. This also means the therapist's time can be used more efficiently by tidying/cleaning the room, rather than having to leave while the guest showers. The treatment surface or receptacle, whether it's a table, tub or dry floatation tank, must be in the center of the room to allow plenty of room for the therapist to access the guest.

In addition, the room will require the following:

- Drainage: Strategically placed floor drain(s) to catch the water run-off from the treatments. Floor drains are in addition to any direct drain connections required by specific pieces of equipment.

- Shower: Treatments may require a shower either before or after so a shower should be in the room or in an adjacent anteroom.

- Sink: Use a "kitchen"-style tap to enable easy filling of bowls that may be used to pour water on the guest during the treatment

- Electricity: Waterproof sockets/receptacles on the floor if the treatment surface/equipment needs power; on the walls for cleaning equipment; and in the cabinetry for any concealed equipment

- Lighting: Indirect, dimmable lighting that is positioned away from the guest's line of vision to prevent them being dazzled

- Ventilation/air conditioning: To maintain a comfortable environment and correct levels of humidity, wet treatment rooms should be heated to 30° C to 35° C

- Floor/wall heating: If used for Turkish massage, then floors and walls should be heated

- Audio and speakers: Either from a central multi-channel system or localized in the room via an MP3 player docking station for a more customized solution. Speaker should be out of the guest's line of sight if recessed into a wall or ceiling.

- Cabinetry/storage: Units are needed to house specialist equipment, such as a hot towel cabinet or hot stone heater; space should be allocated for consumables that are used in various treatments; storage space is needed for clean and soiled linens; and a sink and prep area is usually required.

Structure/Finish: Built or lined using a foam-cored, waterproof, building board prior to receiving finishes, which can be selected from non-porous, fissure-free marble, granite, tile, specialist plasters or custom made, large-format ceramic panels. The finishes should be easily cleaned and suitable for high volumes of water.

Size/Space: The room must accommodate the treatment equipment, all of which will fit into a space of 1.0 m x 2.5 m, with minimum additional circulation space for the therapist at 0.8 m all around the treatment equipment, while allowing space for the shower and cabinetry. An ideal footprint for a room with a separate shower and changing area would be 6.0 m x 2.6 m measured internally.

Hydrotherapy baths can house all the components necessary to run them within the bath itself.

Common Mistakes

- Not paying enough attention to the ergonomics of tables and equipment to create a comfortable experience for both customer and therapist

- Creating difficult to clean areas—instead, make cleaning easy by using flat, smooth surfaces and a removable mattress

- Vichy shower installations must cover a client's entire body—if some areas aren't reached, the client will feel unpleasantly cold

- Forgetting to install a shower in a treatment room that will be used for wraps and mud baths

- Correct delivery of water—both in terms of pressure and temperature

- Residual water remaining on floor due to poor positioning of drains and slope calculation

- Noise can be extremely disturbing during treatments. This has to be kept in mind when planning both the placement of the treatment rooms (e.g., distance to dressing rooms, bar, restaurant) and the interior design of the rooms.

- Ergonomics for both guest and therapist—do everything to make both parties comfortable, such as choosing options like electrical height-adjustable beds

- Incorrect/insufficient electrical installations

- Incorrect positioning of the equipment inside the room

- Not including inspection openings for technical components when integrating equipment into individual design solutions

- Lack of attention to cleaning and disinfection when choosing the equipment

- Insufficient ventilation of the treatment rooms, especially for wet rooms (e.g., equipped with Vichy showers)

- Insufficient amount of space for storing necessary equipment and products

Chapter Four

Pool Areas: Function and Design

The benefits of having a pool or pools—whether full-size lap/exercise pools or vitality pools—in a spa are numerous. "Hydrotherapy" is a term often used to describe the use of water therapy for relaxation, pain relief and treatment. Specially designed pools are a great way to take advantage of the physical properties of water, including temperature and pressure, to promote relaxation and healing of the body.

Pools play a key role in hydrotherapy, promoting relaxation and stress relief.

Hydrotherapy offers a wide array of health benefits, whether combining soothing water temperature with jets and other features for self-massage; using a shock of cold water to stimulate blood circulation; or using the advantage of water for low-impact exercise—the weightlessness of a person's body in water means swimming offers the only way to exercise without a harsh impact on the skeletal system.

This chapter looks closely at how pools work and introduces the reader to the construction and design considerations to be made when adding a pool to a spa or home.

Common Spa Pools

Pool Type	Health & Wellness Benefits	Temp (deg. C)*	Depth	Minimum Water Turnover Rate
Lap/Exercise	• Exercise & fitness • Water aerobics	27 to 29	Variable; 1.0 m to 1.2 m	4 hours
Hydrotherapy/ Vitality	• Massage and relaxation • Increase muscular power • Increase range of joint movement	34 to 40	1.0 m to 1.2m	0.5 to 1.5 hours
Cold Plunge	• Stimulates circulation	12 to 20	1.5 m	20 to 30 minutes
Floatation	• Pain and stress relief	34 to 40	1.0 m to 1.2 m	0.5 to 1.5 hours
Watsu	• Relaxes muscles • Improves mobility	34 to 40	1.0 m to 1.2 m	0.5 to 1.5 hours
Onsen	• Relaxes muscles • Improves mobility	34 to 40	1.0 m to 1.2 m	0.5 to 1.5 hours
Saltwater/ Mineral	• Stress relief • Provides energy to the body • Calms the nervous system • Eliminates/reduces skin irritation • Moisture to the skin	32 to 36	1.0 m to 1.2 m	30 to 90 minutes
Kneipp Walk	• Stimulates circulation • Stress relief • Helps relieve joints	15 to 20 (cold), 30 to 35 (hot)	200 mm to 600mm	0.5 to 1.5 hours

*Temperatures may vary depending on geographical location and if pool is indoor or outdoor.

Lap/Exercise Pool

Lap/Exercise Pool

Temperature: 27° C to 29° C

Depth: Variable; average 1.0 m to 1.2 m

A pool that is large enough to exercise in offers significant benefits. The size of the pool will be determined by the space available and the types of exercising required—for example, different specifications are required for resistance training versus swimming lengths/laps. As a guide, an exercise pool that can accommodate 10 people should be approximately 20 m x 6.5 m x 1.2 m deep, while a traditional lap pool is 25 m long x 12.5 m wide. Where space constraints exist, the use of counter current/swim jets allow on-the-spot exercise.

Benefits

As mentioned previously, swimming is the lowest-impact aerobic exercise available. When the human body is submerged in water, it automatically becomes lighter. In fact, when immersed to the waist, the body bears just 50% of its weight; when immersed to the chest, it reduces to approximately 25% to 35%; when immersed all the way to the neck, the body bears only 10% of its own weight. This type of weightlessness is unattainable any other way.

This means that exercising in a pool is ideal for working stiff muscles and sore joints. The Arthritis Foundation suggests the ideal exercise for relief is one that stretches and strengthens muscles while delivering an aerobic workout—such as doing laps in the pool.

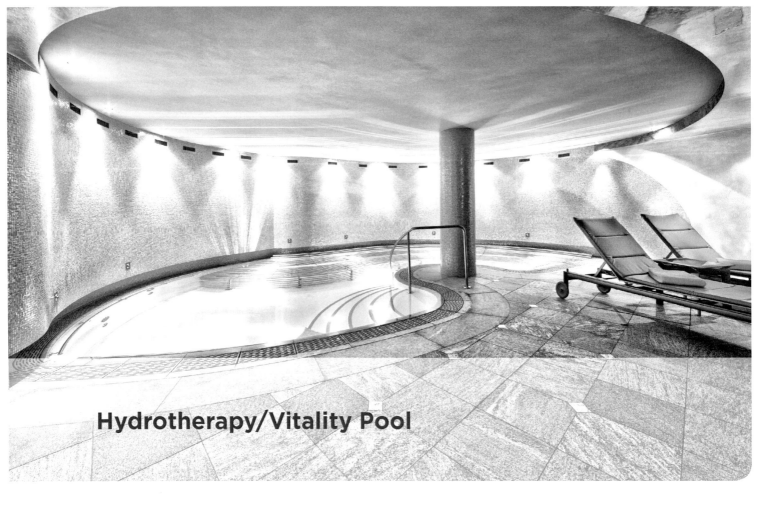

Hydrotherapy/Vitality Pool

Hydrotherapy/Vitality Pool
Temperature: 34° C to 40° C
Depth: 1.0 m to 1.2 m

The combination of warm water (average temperature 38° C) and a selection of water features, including air tubs, swan-neck fountains, air loungers and water jets, means hydrotherapy/vitality pools provide unique benefits, including the cleansing and detoxification of the skin, relieving tired and aching muscles, increasing circulation and relaxing the mind and body.

The difference between the two pools is that hydrotherapy pools are typically much larger than vitality pools and allow guests the ability to "walk" or "float" a course of water features; a vitality pool is more akin to what is often called a "Jacuzzi" (the brand name that has become synonymous with pools with water jets). Vitality pools offer a mini-hydrotherapy experience and are typically used where space will not permit the inclusion of a full-size hydrotherapy pool.

Benefits

These pools deliver true *external* hydrotherapy—the complete immersion of the body in hot water, serving to relax muscles.

Vitality pool features,
like swan-neck
fountain (top); air
recliners (middle)
and air tubs (bottom),
increase relaxation
and stress relief.

Cold Plunge Pool

A cold plunge pool is typically entered after and between hot thermal treatments to cool bathers down.

Going from a heated environment to a cold plunge, which is usually kept at about 10° C to 15° C, stimulates the body in several ways. A quick, 30-second dip is enough to kick start circulation and dilate the vascular system, delivering the positive therapeutic effects of hot/cold contrast therapy.

Benefits

First, the cold water numbs the nerves around joints and muscles. It also causes the release of endorphins and hormones with analgesic properties. Not only does this alleviate some joint pain but muscle aches as well. The cold-water plunge is also believed to stimulate the immune system.

Cold Plunge Pool
Temperature: 5° C to 20° C
Depth: 1.5 m

Onsen Pool

Onsen Pool	
Temperature: 34° C to 40° C	
Depth: 1.0 m to 1.2 m	

This pool originates from Japan—and plays a big role in the country's ritual bathing practices. "*Onsen*" actually translates as "hot springs" in Japanese, but has come to refer to the natural spring baths found throughout Japan.

Traditionally, onsens were used outdoor. They are most often made from Japanese cypress, marble or granite, while indoor tubs are typically constructed of tile, acrylic glass or stainless steel.

Benefits

Since *onsens* use natural hot springs, their benefits are closely dependent on the mineral properties and content of the water itself. But typical benefits include the easing of neuralgia, alleviation of muscle pain and the reduction of the symptoms of chronic skin disease. Onsen bathing is also believed to relieve chronic fatigue and stress.

Specialty Pools

Floatation Pools
Temperature: 34° C to 40° C
Depth: 1.0 m to 1.2 m

Watsu® Pool
Temperature: 34° C to 42° C
Depth: 1.0 m to 1.2 m

Mineral Pool
Temperature: 32° C to 36° C
Depth: 1.0 m to 1.2 m

Kneipp Walk
Temperature: 15° C to 20° C (cold) and
30° C to 35° C (hot)
Depth: 200 mm to 250 mm

Floatation Pools

Temperature: 34° C to 40° C
Depth: 1.0 m to 1.2 m

A floatation pool or tank is usually enclosed and typically measures approximately 2.5 m long x 1.2 m wide. The water in the tank is around 25 cm deep and is kept at body temperature. The most important element of the tank is the addition of magnesium sulfate (Epsom salt) that is dissolved in the tank: approximately 400 kg of Epsom salt to 200 gallons of water—this is what creates the weightless "float." As opposed to a swimming pool where there is a sense of weightlessness, gravity in a floatation tank is completely nullified by the buoyancy caused by the dissolved Epsom salt.

Unique to the enclosed floatation tanks is the sensory deprivation they provide. This restricted stimulation has been proven to change the way the brain works, showing an increase in theta waves in the brain[1]—the waves that are activated by meditation and active during REM sleep.

Socializing plays a very important role in hydrothermal bathing. Here guests enjoy the mineral pool at Peninsula Hot Springs, Victoria, Australia.

Benefits

The increase in theta waves is thought to reduce stress and encourage a happy, contented brain. The physical benefits of floating in magnesium sulfate also gives those that suffer from joint and/or muscle pain huge relief by taking away the effects of gravity on the body. There is also the innate benefit of absorbing the Epsom salt through the skin, which is full of magnesium, something many people are deficient in. Raising magnesium levels can improve circulation, ease muscle pain and relieve stress[2].

Watsu® Pool

Temperature: 34° C to 40° C
Depth: 1.0 m to 1.2 m

These are pools designed specifically for Watsu massage, a gentle form of body therapy performed in warm water. It combines elements of massage, joint mobilization, shiatsu, muscle stretching and dance. The receiver is continuously supported while being floated, cradled, rocked and stretched. This typically requires a 3.5-meter diameter pool for single treatments, and a larger pool if the desire is to give simultaneous treatments.

Benefits

Watsu massage is designed to induce a state of deep relaxation to the body and the mind and relieve stress.

Because it's such a gentle treatment, it's also good for the elderly and children. The weightlessness effect of the water provides for gentle stretching and joint mobilization. This treatment is often used to treat different conditions like brain injury, stroke, spinal cord injury, Parkinson's disease, cerebral palsy, arthritis and fibromyalgia. It is also used to treat chronic pain and in post-surgical or post-trauma recoveries.

Mineral Pool

Temperature: 32° C to 36° C
Depth: 1.0 m to 1.2 m

Mineral pools come in all shapes and sizes—they can be full size pools, wading pools or vitality pools. The water temperature of mineral baths may be hot, warm, cool or even cold. Mineral waters can have an acidic, basic or neutral pH, depending on the types of dissolved solids in the water. Some mineral waters contain arsenic or other toxic substances and should never be used for drinking water, unless specified that it is all right to do so.

Benefits

Throughout the centuries, mineral spas and pools have been enjoyed on many levels, including for cleansing, social and health benefits. Today, the healing benefits of the natural mineral springs are well-known and usage of hot springs is on the rise.

Kneipp Walk

Temperature: 15° C to 20° C and 30° C to 35° C
Depth: 200 mm to 250 mm

The Kneipp walk is a water treatment using a mix of hot and cold water actions (stepping through the water) to stimulate the metabolism of tissues and the circulation of blood. Pebbles on the bottom of the stream/walkway massage the feet, and the alternation of hot and cold baths stimulate circulation of all parts of the body.

There are two walks used—the bather begins by stepping in hot water for one minute to two minutes (the water is usually lit up with color), and then moves to the cold-water pool (usually lit light blue) for half a minute. The process is repeated approximately three times. A handrail is often used to help the bather walk through the different water pressures. Kneipp walks can be located anywhere within the spa journey and are often used as a feature by designers, creating interesting paths and walkways.

Benefits

Kneipp therapy was created in the 19th century by Sebastian Kneipp, a Bavarian parish priest, who fell ill with tuberculosis and strongly believed that his use of a "water cure" healed him. Kneipp therapy is well-respected and even subsidized by the government in some European countries for both preventative and rehabilitative purposes. Kneipp therapy does not have to take place in a pool—in fact, hot and cold compresses can be used—but pools are most common.

Applications of hot and cold water have long been used to cure headaches, improve lymphatic function and even eliminate hangovers. Kneipp walks are often used in treatment for conditions from arthritis, abscesses and heart disease to asthma, diabetes and allergic eczema.

Kneipp walks use hot and cold water to stimulate circulation and overall wellbeing.

A well-designed pool is an aesthetically-pleasing focal point.

Pool Area Design

When designing pool areas, it is important to remember that people interact differently when minimally clothed. This means there is an increased need for personal space.

Special consideration should be given to corridors, passageways and circulation spaces where guests travel in opposite directions. Pinch-points should be avoided, and poolside relaxation spaces should be designed with personal space in mind. If there is food or beverage service offered in these areas, than space for staff to attend to guests and tables for service items should be provided.

In addition, benches and seats in the pools need to allow for adequate space between bodies (600 mm is recommended); where possible, it's advised to provide individual seating so that bathers don't have to consider invading another's personal space on a communal bench. Seats should also be shaped to allow for comfort and space where air jets might push the bather away from the seat back.

To create a bather-friendly environment, pools should also have sufficiently wide treads and short risers for entries and exits and no sudden drops at the junction with the floor.

Access for Persons with Disabilities

- The route to the pool must not be confusing and lead directly through a shower area.

- Handrails should be provided between the changing rooms and poolside, and tactile information must be placed at critical points on circulation routes.

- Design and detailing at the pool edge is critical to warn swimmers they are approaching the pool edge.

- The minimum water depth to provide sufficient buoyancy for adult disabled swimmers is 1,200 mm. However, learner pools should be accessible to disabled children and other groups who may prefer a shallower depth of water.

- Moveable floors can be particularly useful in learner pools, as they provide the deeper water necessary for adult swimmers with a lower-limb disability.

- Disabled swimmers can access the pool by a variety of means with a ramped entry or hoist being the minimum requirement.

- Floor finishes must be reliable and slip-resistant with a non-abrasive surface.

Surface Finishes

Surface finishes for pools should be selected based upon several criteria: safety, hygiene, ease of maintenance and visual appearance. Natural stone is a popular finish in pool areas; however, these don't carry slip-resistance ratings like manufactured tile finishes. Natural finishes, such as slate, should be carefully selected, as many varieties have a tendency to de-laminate, and any marble finishes with fissures should be avoided. Limestone, in all its various forms, should generally be avoided in wet areas, as it is not only very soft and easily eroded, but species like Travertine can be very heavily fissured. Even though these tiles can be supplied with fissures filled with a resin-based material, new openings will inevitably form during use.

If choosing natural stone, it's important to use a testing agency to test slippage. The cost for this is minimal and is highly recommended, as it demonstrates due diligence. Of course, it's also imperative to choose floor surfaces that minimize the potential for slippage and use the correct sloping angle[3] for proper drainage. It's worth noting that the requirement for non-slip surfaces is only in critical areas, including the treads of the steps and the top of the slope inside the pool down to the deeper areas.

Pool Types

The aesthetics of a pool are very much affected by the type of pool chosen. There are two types of pools: overflow and freeboard. An overflow pool is most commonly chosen for hydrotherapy spas because they can be level with the decking or designed as infinity pools. On the other hand, in a freeboard/skimmer pool, the water level is approximately 150 mm below the pool deck, creating a visible edge.

Not only do the pools look very different, but they also function differently in terms of how they handle the

Indoor pool at Tschuggen Grand Hotel, Arosa, Switzerland.

treatment and flow of pool water. An overflow pool uses a balance tank to store and treat the overflow of surface water that runs off when people get into the pool. The displaced water is captured, treated and then pumped back into the pool. A skimmer pool, instead, does not have the inherent benefit of constantly renewing its surface water because the displacement is handled by the water level rising versus vacating the pool.

This means overflow pools are very efficient when it comes to removing and treating polluted surface water. This is important because surface water, which holds approximately 75% of a pool's pollution, is often ingested by swimmers.

Design Considerations

Pools are complex to build and manage. User safety, efficient water treatment and pleasing aesthetics start with careful planning, specification and design.

The water treatment system must be an integral part of the architectural, structural, mechanical and electrical design of the building. It is critical at the earliest stages of a project, after determining the type of pool(s) being installed, to consider the following key factors:

- Anticipated bather load (required to determine pool and plant sizing)
- Pool size and volume (length x width x depth), plus any hydrotherapy equipment to be incorporated into the pool
- Pool location
- Balance tank location
- Plant room location and size
- Level of pool, balance tank and plant room are of paramount importance

Pool Tank/Basin Construction

Pool tanks or basins (the pool structure itself) can be built from various materials, including concrete, stainless steel or fiberglass. There are some functional and aesthetic differences between these materials.

Concrete: A common, affordable choice, but pools rendered in concrete can suffer from water leakage.

Common Mistakes

- Chemical smells permeating nearby areas
- Floor slippery and dangerous
- Bulbs in the pool difficult to replace
- Poor overflow drainage
- Inadequate filtration and water treatment plant space
- Insufficient provision of MEP services—power, water, drainage etc.
- Inadequate water turnover rates leading to poor water quality
- Adopting high filtration rates leading to poor water quality
- Lack of secondary disinfection (e.g. UV) leading to excessive chemicals in the pool
- Poor provision for the delivery of chemicals to the plant room

It's important to conduct a percolation test to ensure water integrity before tiling a pool built from concrete.

Stainless Steel: Popular for both its aesthetic value and water retention ability. A minimum grade 316L stainless steel, which is more resistant to corrosion than conventional stainless steel, should be used for freshwater pools. If the pool is saltwater, a higher grade of stainless steel is required. Modular stainless steel is also an option. Here, the stainless steel panels have a PVC lining. The modular design makes them quick to construct and removes the need for hot welding on site.

Fiberglass or Glass Reinforced Plastic: Offer great water retention and can be delivered as a single piece or in sections for construction on site.

Pre-Formed, Composite Shell: A next-generation pool structure. Pre-formed, composite shells combine three materials working together to create a bespoke, tiled pool that is quick and easy to install. Pool shells are manufactured out of fiberglass with an epoxy-laminate layer to ensure waterproofing and finished in a ceramic mosaic tile; finally, the fully finished pool is delivered directly to the site, ready for installation

Pool Finishes

Pools are usually finished in tiles, either mosaic or larger format. And non-slip tiles are essential around stairs and shallow areas. Natural stone or slate is not recommended because it is porous and can discolor, leaving a residue on the pool floor. If considering such materials, test them with pool chemicals prior to installation.

In order to increase waterproofing, a rendered finish can be used. The rendered finish is applied between the concrete structure and the finish tile.

Stainless steel pools are usually left bare (versus tiled) and can be polished to produce either a satin-brushed or mirror finish.

PVC liners are often used in large, public pools where there's a need for an affordable pool finish that is watertight. These flexible membranes can be applied to both concrete and stainless steel pools. They come in various colors.

Pollution and Cleaning

Pollution in swimming pools' water comes from many sources; however, swimmers themselves are the major source. In fact, it is said that each swimmer can introduce as much as 600 million bacteria into the pool! In addition to bacteria, there are other pollutants caused by swimmers, like perspiration, cosmetics, suntan lotion, hair products, sweat, urine, etc.

Interestingly, the chemicals used to treat pool water can also create their own problems. A key mistake in water treatment is when an operator uses five or six chemicals to keep the water in balance. These can include: sodium hypochlorite acid (for pH correction), sodium bicarbonate (for alkalinity adjustment), alum (as a filter aid), calcium flake (for grout protection)

Guide to Pool Pollution

Surface Pollution: Hair, dust, grease, excreta, floating debris, grass, etc. This can often be handled by an efficient surface draw-off system, such as those found in level-deck pools. Of course, larger items of surface debris can be removed by the pool staff.

Dissolved Pollution: Urine, perspiration, cosmetics, etc. Efficient filtration and circulation is critical for treatment, as well as maintaining sufficient chlorine levels for breaking it down.

Suspended-Matter Pollution: Water treatment and cleaning chemicals. To deal with these, use the minimum quantities of chemicals in and around the pool and maintain carefully balanced water.

Insoluble Pollution: Fluff, dirt, precipitated chemicals, filter sand, etc. Sweep or vacuum the pool bottom daily or as required.

and sodium thiosulphate (used for over chlorination). Scum line cleaners and poolside cleaners can also find their way into the pool.

With careful management and selection of the correct sanitizer, as few as two or three chemicals can do the same job with better results.

How Pools Operate

When considering the installation of a pool, it's important to understand how they work, especially in regards to filtration and water treatment.

All the pool water must be filtered and treated to keep the pool safe and clean—and determining how long it takes to move the entire contents of a pool through the filter system is called "turnover rate." The turnover rate required helps determine the pool pump that is needed. A higher-use pool with more water will require

Overflow:
Level Deck

Pool water is level with the pool surroundings. Aesthetically pleasing and inherently cleaner because most of the polluted surface water flows over the edge of the pool into the transfer channel connected to the balance tank.

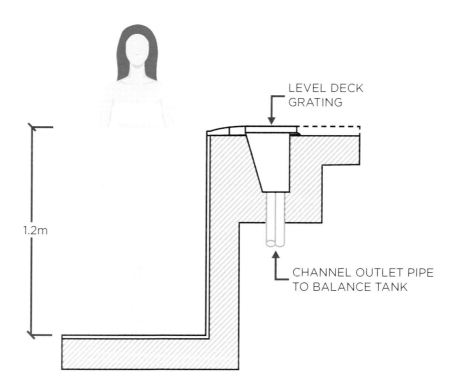

LEVEL DECK
GRATING

1.2m

CHANNEL OUTLET PIPE
TO BALANCE TANK

Overflow:
Infinity Edge

Similar to level-deck pool, but the water is transferred to an overhanging channel and gives the visual appearance of the pool water blending (merging) with the horizon.

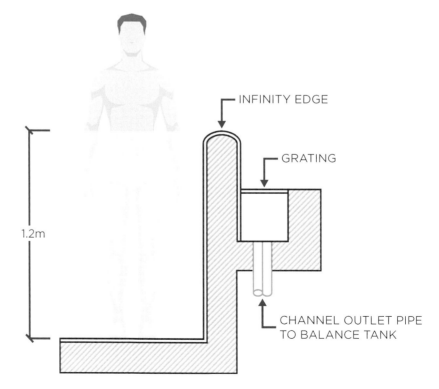

INFINITY EDGE

GRATING

1.2m

CHANNEL OUTLET PIPE
TO BALANCE TANK

Freeboard:
Skimmer

Space between the
water level and the top
of the pool deck.

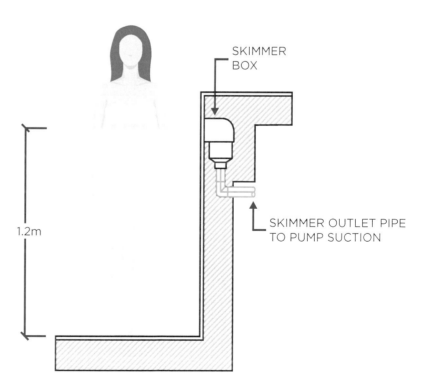

SKIMMER
BOX

1.2m

SKIMMER OUTLET PIPE
TO PUMP SUCTION

Filtration Water Treatment Flow

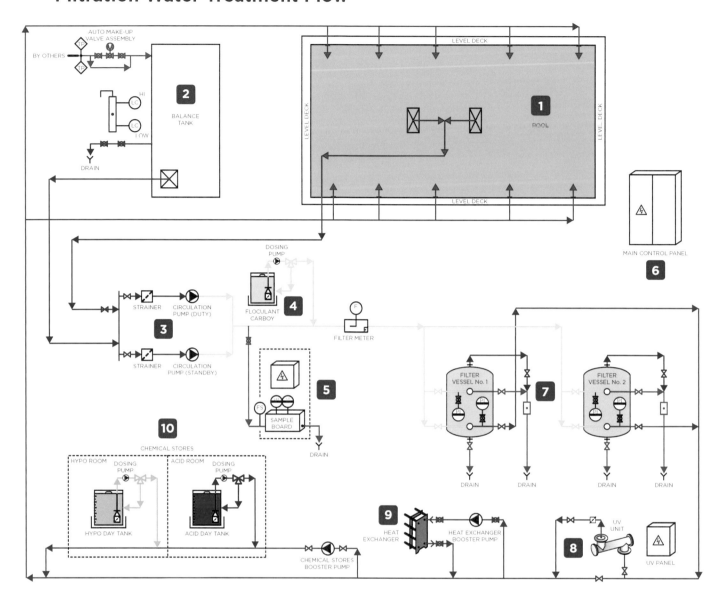

1 – Pool Tank/Basin

The pool illustrated here is a typical level-deck pool with concentric bottom-sump outlets and wall inlets evenly positioned to provide the best possible water distribution. It is recommended that outlets have a maximum velocity of 0.5 m/second for suction and 0.5 m to 1.0 m/second for inlets. All pool fittings should be designed in compliance with international pool entrapment standards, which means no gap greater than 8 mm. In larger pools, it's recommended to include vacuum points for pool cleaning so automatic

pool cleaners can clean the pool overnight.

2 – Balance Tank

Balance tanks are required for all overflow pools in order to contain the "surge" caused by bather displacement, whether level deck, infinity edge or other variation. Bathers entering the pool displace water to the overflow system, which feeds pool water to the balance tank. This effectively drops the pool water level.

Fresh water is introduced into the system via an auto make-up system in the balance tank and the pool inlets return the height of the pool water to normal.

3 – Circulating Pumps

Main circulating pumps are at the heart of the filtration system, and their selection is crucial to the continuous operation of the filtration and water treatment system. Upstream of the main circulation pumps, strainers should be fitted to protect the pumps from any pool debris. (These should be inspected and cleaned on a weekly basis.)

4 – Flocculation Dosing System

Incorporating the continuous dosing of a coagulant in very small quantities is an effective way to remove microscopic impurities and organisms from a pool, including common waterborne parasites, like cryptosporidium, the germ that causes diarrhea.

5 – Chemical Controller

Monitors and regulates pool chemical levels.

6 – Electrical Control Panel

Electrical control panels are required to provide power to all of the electrical equipment in the plant room and to provide overload protection to the equipment. The electrical control panel can also be linked to the Building Management System, providing fault signals to a central control room.

7 – Filtration

Good filtration is essential for ensuring water quality. The most common filtration method for commercial usage is medium-rate, vertical sand filters, but there is also regenerative, diatomaceous earth and cartilage filtration to consider. Of critical importance is the filtration rate—the higher the rate, the lower the filtration efficiency. *Note: Filtration rates should not exceed 25m3/m2/hour (flow rate/area of flow rate/time).*

8 – Secondary Disinfection

It is strongly recommended to have a secondary disinfection process in place to fight waterborne parasites. There are several options available:

• Full Ozone: Ozone gas is used to complement chlorination and results in lower levels of chlorine; however this requires a good level of expertise to operate, additional space in the plant room and is more expensive to install and run.

• Ultra-violet (UV): Commonly used to complement chlorination and allows pools to operate with lower levels of chlorine.

• Partial-Flow UV or Ozone: an alternative when there are space restrictions as only a 10% to 25% of total flow rate is treated so not as effective as full-flow treatments.

9 – Pool Heating

Common methods of heating are gas and/or oil boilers; electrical heating; heat exchanger (particularly used in very hot countries).

10 – Chemical Injection

Automatic chemical dosing systems are recommended

Pool Chemical Primer

Disinfectants

• Sodium Hypochlorite: Supplied in liquid form either in small pack or bulk with a maximum chlorine strength of 15%. Widely used in pools where hard water is the source water.

• Calcium Hypochlorite: Supplied in granular and tablet form with a maximum chlorine strength of 65% to 68%. Most often used in pools where soft water is the source water.

• Bromine: Supplied in granular or tablet form, bromine is an alternative to chlorine. Though closely related, bromine is able to withstand heat better than chlorine so is recommended for spa pools, but isn't ideal for larger commercial pools.

pH Correction

• Sodium Bisulphate: Supplied as a dry powder to be mixed in water.

• Hydrochloric Acid: Supplied in concentrated liquid form, requires dilution and is very gaseous.

• Sulphuric Acid: Supplied in concentrated liquid form, requires dilution. An exothermic reaction occurs when added to water.

• CO_2 Gas: Supplied in either small pack container or bulk, this product is not advisable to be used within a pool that has air features, as the gas will escape into the atmosphere while the water is agitated, reducing the effectiveness of the CO_2 gas and making the control of the PH difficult to manage.

where possible.

Plant Room Design

Plant rooms need to be considered in the very early stages of the design process. There are numerous reasons for this—including the fact that they will invariably take up more space than operators might anticipate. They also require input from a structural engineer to ensure that the foundation is capable of holding the weight of the balance tank and filtration and water treatment plant. And, finally, plant rooms must be situated in areas that allow for the minimizing of noise and vibration.

Plant Room Design Considerations

Foundation: A structural engineer should ensure that plant room slab is capable of holding the working

weight of the balance tank and filtration and water treatment plant.

Noise Reduction: Plant rooms should be strategically located to keep noise to a minimum in other areas of the spa. In addition, every effort should be made to minimize noise and vibration. For example, typical equipment noise levels for main circulating pumps are >80dbA, and air blowers are >85dbA. Insulated acoustic panels and/or doors should be incorporated.

Drainage: Gullies are required for main circulating pump strainers, filters, chemical rooms and chemical controllers/sample boards. In addition, a dedicated back-wash connection is recommended for each filter.

Level: Plant room slab level needs to be a minimum of one meter below the pool static water level. If this is not possible, than a pump pit should be incorporated into the plant room. Should the drainage level be higher

---

Water Hydraulics

For effective water hydraulics, the levels of the pool static water, balance tank and main circulating pumps are of critical importance; examples of good design are shown here.

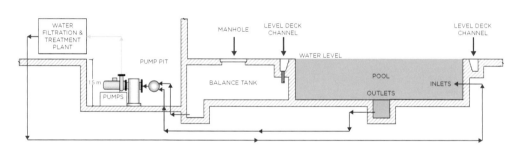

Option 1: Pool Water Treatment Plant on Same Level as Pool

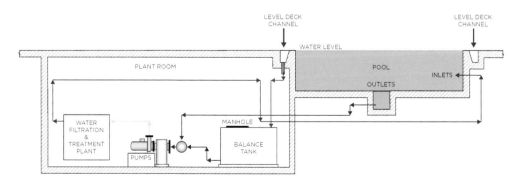

Option 2: Pool Water Treatment Plant & Balance Tank on Level Below

than the pit, a recess sump should be incorporated and an automatic sump pump installed to drain.

Space: The amount of space required to house the pool filtration and water treatment plant vary considerably depending on the number and size of pools being built. Table 4:2 is supplied as a guide for spa whirlpools and vitality pools.

Health/Safety: The filtration plant room must be designed in accordance with published guidelines (e.g., Pool Water Treatment Advisory Group), and the water treatment plant arranged in accordance with good standard practice. Adequate provision has to be made for safe daily operator access and for effective and efficient ongoing service and maintenance of the entire system.

Work plinths may be required to provide access to all of the filtration and water treatment plant.

Lighting/Power: Adequate lighting and power supply outlets are necessary throughout plant and chemical rooms and should meet local/international requirements.

Ventilation/Temperature: The minimum number of air changes required in the plant room is four per hour. The temperature should not fall below 10° C or rise above 30° C.

Pool Lighting

Halogen*
Currently being phased out in most countries because they are less energy efficient.

LED*
Offer longer life and varying color options; various size and styles of fitting available (flush, beveled, frosted glass, strip lighting, stainless steel bezel, etc.).

Fiber Optics
Provides lower level of illumination but offer unrivalled effects. Can create moods and sensations that cannot be achieved with most other lighting systems. Because fiber-optic lights contain no heat or electricity, they are well-suited for use in pools. They are also easier to maintain, as there is no "bulb" to replace; instead an illuminator or projector transmits the light through the fiber. This "remote light projector" can be located conveniently for bulb replacement.

*Halogen and LED lights must have an IP68 rating—this is the highest Ingress Protection rating and means they are protected against complete, continuous submersion in water.

....

[1] http://floatforhealth.net/suedfeld.pdf
[2] http://www.epsomsaltcouncil.org/articles/universal_health_institute_about_epsom_salt.pdf
[3] Refer to the German DIN 51097 standard and aim for the classification "B" (least slippery); another respected standard to follow is the British Standard Pendulum Test BS 7976-2 and BS 13036-4

Space

Pool (L x W x D)	Volume	Balance Tank (L x W x D)	Plant Room (L x W x D)	Area
3 m Dia	3 m³	1.5 m x 1.0 m x 1.0 m	3.5 m x 3.0 m x 2.5 m	10.5 m²
5.0 m x 4.0 m x 1.2 m	25 m³	4.0 m x 1.2 m x 1.0 m	5.0 m x 2.5 m x 2.5 m	12.5 m²
7.0 m x 6.0 m x 1.2 m	50 m³	6.0 m x 1.5 m x 1.0 m	6.5 m x 4.5 m x 2.5 m	30.0 m²

Note: Maximum required height of full-ozone plants must be over 3 m.

Chapter Five

Building Services

This chapter covers the major elements in the engineering and management of a hydrothermal spa. It's designed to give readers a closer look at the "behind-the-scenes" operations that bring a spa design to a working reality, including the ventilation, drainage, electrical services and lighting. The choices made in building services also play a key role in the overall environmental impact of a building—something that is relevant both in domestic and commercial builds of hydrothermal areas.

With the help of a Building Management System, spas should be able to run and monitor most of the functions of their hydrothermal area right from the front desk.

Please note, this chapter is meant as a general guideline to these complex areas, and it's important to work with specialists who have local knowledge on the standards and codes to follow.

Ventilation and Climate Control

Regardless of the type of thermal room or cabin— sauna, steam bath, hamam, relaxation room, etc.— proper ventilation and climate control are crucial to the bathers' comfort and health and significantly impact the effectiveness of the thermal room. An heating, ventilation, air conditioning (HVAC) contractor must be engaged for this purpose and will work closely with the mechanical and electrical (M&E) consultant.

Key to proper ventilation is the supply of oxygen to the room—this is vital in artificially heated environments. Low oxygen levels will result in bathers feeling or even becoming truly unwell, including fainting or worse. In addition, proper ventilation will promote drying of the

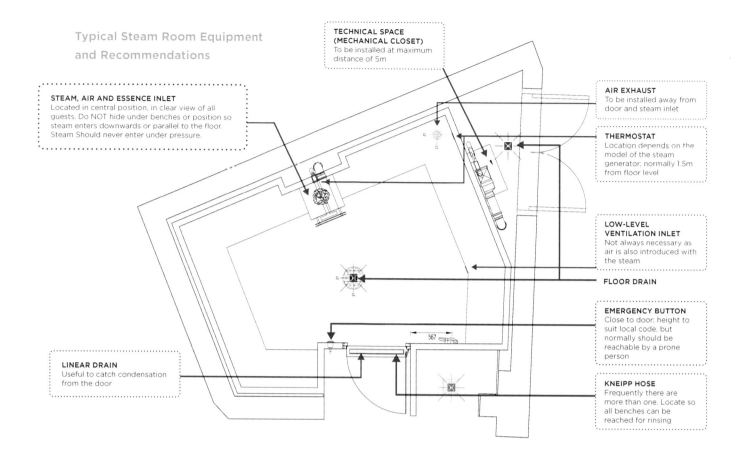

**TECHNICAL SPACE
(MECHANICAL CLOSET)**
To be installed at maximum
distance of 5m

STEAM, AIR AND ESSENCE INLET
Located in central position, in clear view of all
guests. Do NOT hide under benches or position so
steam enters downwards or parallel to the floor.
Steam Should never enter under pressure.

AIR EXHAUST
To be installed away from
door and steam inlet

THERMOSTAT
Location depends on the
model of the steam
generator; normally 1.5m
from floor level

**LOW-LEVEL
VENTILATION INLET**
Not always necessary as
air is also introduced with
the steam

FLOOR DRAIN

EMERGENCY BUTTON
Close to door; height to
suit local code, but
normally should be
reachable by a prone
person

LINEAR DRAIN
Useful to catch condensation
from the door

KNEIPP HOSE
Frequently there are
more than one. Locate so
all benches can be
reached for rinsing

rooms. Mold, fungus and bacteria spores easily grow in warm, moist environments so correctly engineered ventilation will aid in the drying out of the cabins and will minimize the health risks associated with these microorganisms.

As well, ventilation is what keeps the rooms at optimum bathing temperatures and ensures correct levels of humidity are produced for the maximum benefit (especially important in a steam room). When a cabin is not run at the correct temperature or does not provide the right humidity level, the experience will not meet bathers' expectations.

The materials used to build cabins have a significant effect on the efficiency of the room and how easy or difficult it is to maintain the correct climate. If traditional building materials like concrete, blocks or drywall are used, there will be a greater likelihood that the steam generation will not function correctly. The use of efficient building materials, such as a coated

foam board that provides maximum waterproofing and thermal insulation, increases the effectiveness of the steam generator. Even then, there will be a level of radiant heat reflected back into the room from the wall and floor finishes, which will usually be some form of tile or stone that will require ventilation.

If not ventilated properly, radiant heat can upset the temperature/steam balance. Because steam rooms and other humid/wet cabins require varying levels of humidity to be artificially created by steam generators, they rely on temperature probes or sensors (hygrometers) to activate the steam. If the sensors can't detect the correct temperature because of too much heat in the room or because they are placed in an incorrect location (e.g., too high)—usually caused by overheating the walls and benches or using inferior construction materials that absorb and emit too much heat—then the temperature/steam balance becomes unsettled, and the room is not able to function as it should.

The placement of temperature sensors needs particular attention. They are usually located approximately 1.5 m from the floor (which is the approximate height of a person's head—and the most sensitive part of the body—when sitting on a bench), and, because the sensors penetrate the walls, they are susceptible to high levels of heat being radiated from the structure of the walls.

Professional steam generators can operate inlet and exhaust fans automatically to maintain and regulate the optimum cabin climate. For example, the exhaust fan will not be switched on until the cabin reaches the desired temperature. It will then extract the condensation heat accumulation until the steam bath temperature drops below the set point, which switches the generator on again.

An overrun program (drying program) keeps inlet and outlet fans running for a period after the unit is switched into standby mode. This ensures complete evacuation of the steam and assists in the cooling and drying out of the cabin.

Common Mistakes

- Not making provision for increased air distribution around hotter temperature pools (e.g., vitality pools) and treatment plant rooms. HVAC consultant must pay close attention to the temperatures of the pools.

- Not having correct water pressure and flow rate to operate experience showers, jet showers, Vichy showers, etc.

- Not choosing a steam generator based on the quality of the local water—hard water or soft water require different systems

- Not considering that materials used for ventilation ducts have to be non-corrosive

Ductwork must be made of a non-corrosive material— plastic, aluminum or stainless steel—and ducting must be smooth to avoid condensation.

Proper ventilation in the pool area helps minimize evaporation and controls condensation. In addition, it removes chlorine smells and other contaminants from the air and creates a comfortable environment for bathers, staff and spectators. Pool areas are generally kept between 24° C to 28° C, but this also depends on the time of year, the temperatures of the pools in the area, etc. Getting this right is critical to bather comfort, and it is imperative that the HVAC specialist and wet area specialist work together to calculate the fresh air and air changes required, as well as the temperature that needs to be maintained in this area.

Because of the higher operating temperatures in the pool area, evaporation is a key consideration when planning climate control and ventilation. Some general evaporation principles to be aware of:

- Larger water surfaces result in a greater evaporation and condensation. *Use a pool cover where possible.*

- Higher water temperature = higher rate of evaporation

- Lower indoor air temperature = higher rate of evaporation

- Lower indoor relative humidity = higher rate of evaporation

- Greater air movement = higher rate of evaporation

Note that there is a theory that condensation can be significantly minimized if the air temperature is kept 1° C to 2° C higher than that of the temperature of the pool. However, this does NOT work for vitality pools which are usually kept at 36° C. The air temperature will become far too hot if it's raised even just 1° higher.

Thermal Cabin Ventilation

Typical Duct and Air Valve Materials

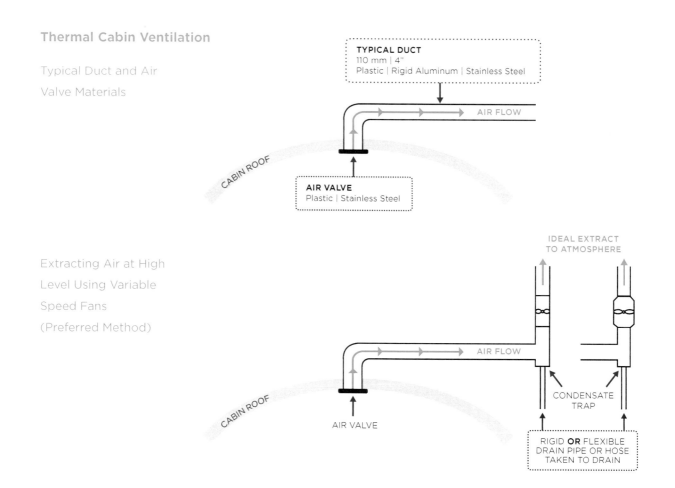

TYPICAL DUCT
110 mm | 4"
Plastic | Rigid Aluminum | Stainless Steel

AIR FLOW

CABIN ROOF

AIR VALVE
Plastic | Stainless Steel

Extracting Air at High Level Using Variable Speed Fans (Preferred Method)

IDEAL EXTRACT TO ATMOSPHERE

AIR FLOW

CABIN ROOF

AIR VALVE

CONDENSATE TRAP

RIGID **OR** FLEXIBLE DRAIN PIPE OR HOSE TAKEN TO DRAIN

Air and Heat Extraction Tips

Wet area specialists are well-versed in accepted standards of air and heat extraction and can advise the HVAC consultant. It's important to follow these general guidelines:

- Exhaust ductwork must be made of a non-corrosive material—plastic, aluminum or stainless steel, depending on local building department regulations and codes. Moist air, often mixed with the essence of essential oils, can be very corrosive.

- Exhaust ducting must be smooth, not flexible, to avoid condensation.

- Exhaust ducting must always fall in the direction of a condensate drain point, which should be at the lowest point in the ductwork. If necessary, more than one drain point should be provided. It is vital that all risks of pooling or lying water be removed to prevent the incubation of Legionella (the bacteria that causes legionnaire's disease, a severe form of pneumonia).

- Correct balancing of the ventilation system requires each cabin to have its own inlet and exhaust fans.

- If individual fans are not used, an electrical or manually operated volume-control damper should be installed within the duct.

- Fans should provide four to six air changes per hour and have variable speed controllers to balance airflow and ensure a slight negative air pressure in the room.

- Inlet and exhaust ducts in rooms terminate in plastic or stainless steel grilles or air valves—these are NOT intended to replace fans or volume-control dampers.

- Avoid painted or coated aluminum grilles, as the coating invariably peels off.

- Fans should be installed in a vertical section of the duct wherever possible.

- If fan is of a larger diameter than the duct, it is mandatory that it is fitted in a vertical section of the duct to avoid water condensing in the fan housing.

- Condensate traps and drains for thermal rooms

Land Vs. Maritime Construction

Recognizing the huge trend towards putting spa facilities on boats and cruise ships, here are some considerations to make when building wet areas that will be at sea:

- Building standards/codes for ships are set by IMO-International Maritime Organization, not other standards mentioned in this handbook

- Fire safety and smoke minimization is critical - far more so than for land-based projects

- Thermal cabins must be constructed in aluminum sheet - using the traditional "dry wall" system of metal framing, but replacing gypsum board with a single aluminum sheet on the outside, fiberglass insulation in the core and a twin-wall aluminum sheet on the inside

- Walls must then be sealed and waterproofed with resin compound and bondage

are not standard pieces of equipment available "off the shelf" from HVAC equipment suppliers—the HVAC contractor should have a specialist ductwork fabricator manufacture suitable components.

Note: Local and/or national building codes also must be considered.

It is important to balance the ventilation system to ensure a slight negative pressure to minimize the loss of steam/climate. This will not, however, be able to completely stop steam being sucked out of the cabin, so it is vitally important that the HVAC contractor installs an exhaust point directly above the door, to the exterior of the cabin. This positioning is ideal because an exhaust point further away will draw the escaping hot, humid air along the ceiling and, the further it is drawn, the more it will condense and cause drips. This often causes considerable damage to ceilings, which

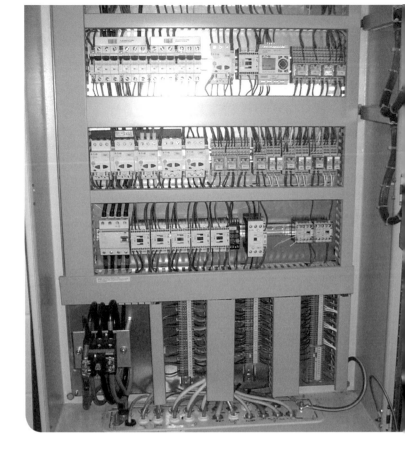

Electrical services are incredibly complex in today's spas; it's important to consult with an M&E specialist during the planning phase to insure there is enough electricity available.

will not have been constructed in materials or with finishes to withstand constant exposure to moisture.

Electrical Services

In today's hydrothermal spas, the electrical load required for all the specialist equipment is extensive. For example, the steam generator and sauna heater are typically electrically driven, as are the mood lighting systems featured in thermal cabins and pools, just to name a few. Electrical planning, therefore, forms an important part of the overall planning of a wet spa, especially when you also consider the in-room extras like electronically adjusted massage tables and specialist treatment devices. The amount of ampere or kilowatts required and the distribution of that power require consultation between an M&E consultant and a wet area specialist.

Of course, if the building has limited access to electricity for any reason (such as electriciy is cost-prohibitive or the location is far from the power source), understanding and planning for the electrics at the earliest stages is even more crucial. If electricity is in short supply, there are alternatives that can be considered, such as heating pools using a heat

exchanger or using traditional wood burning stoves in a sauna.

Because thermal rooms feature the use of heat and water, safety requirements are paramount when it comes to the electrical components and fittings. They need to be protected from both these elements through the use of waterproofing, correct heat shielding and the selection of fittings, as required by the needs of the installation.

When placing electrical socket outlets in wet treatment rooms, they should be in housings or mounting systems that are in compliance with national electrical codes. When sourcing the treatment equipment that will be using these sockets, ensure they can be locally transformed to 12/24V to minimize risk.

All wet-area electrical outlets should be protected by residual current devices that are designed to trip quickly if any water ingress causes leakage of current to earth/ground. It is important to earth/ground-metal-framed equipment; furniture and plumbing must also be earth/ground-bonded in wet areas. This also applies to metal door frames.

Often omitted in design are power sockets required for cleaning equipment. These, ideally, should be placed outside the room or within built-in cabinetry in the room. In a multi-function room where multiple treatments require varying electrical equipment, the equipment should be housed in cabinetry and the sockets enclosed within the cabinets.

Some countries have restrictions on electrical sockets being at a set distance, often 2.0 m, from a water source. This can be particularly restrictive if plug-in equipment is required for treatment preparations, so care should be taken in planning the preparation area to ensure a cabinet-mounted socket is within reach.

Electrical equipment within thermal rooms, e.g., sauna stoves, lamps and lighting, is normally manufactured, tested and certificated as safe for use in the environment in which it is to be used. This is why sourcing equipment from specialist manufacturers is essential. In many countries, safety codes differ between commercial and residential properties so care should be taken that, in all instances, only professional-duty products are used.

As the electrical services are a major installation, the relevant circuit boxes, breakers and other system components need to be installed and maintained.

Electrical Equipment Found in Wet Treatment and Thermal Rooms, Includes:

- Aromatization/fragrance blower
- Fragrance pump (pump for single/multiple fragrances)
- Brine solution pump (pump for sterile brine solution spray)
- Bubbling system (for foot baths)
- Foam generator (for hamam massage)
- Infrared heat lamps
- Lighting—ceiling LEDs, ceiling lights over treatment tables, wall sconces, under-bench strip lights and control units for light programs, including transformers
- MP3 player
- Speakers
- Steam generator
- Steam shower
- Sauna heater
- Control panels
- Panic/emergency button connected to an external alarm

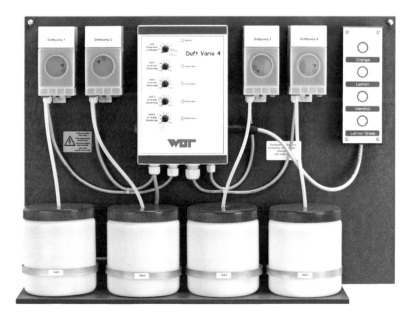

Fragrance pumps can power multiple aromas.

All electrical work should be carried out by qualified persons and in accordance with local regulations and permit requirements.

Drainage

This is one of the key components of a successful wet-room installation, as it has implications for maintenance, cleaning, health and safety. The drainage system is in place to remove water from all sources (taps, shower heads, hoses, condensation, etc.) and will also facilitate the cleaning and washing down of an area. The quantity and positioning of waste drains is key to efficient drainage, as are the quality of fittings—which can corrode quickly if sufficiently robust materials are not used.

Multiple drains may be required depending on the floor area and the equipment used—for example, steam generators will require separate drainage from the waste outlet.

Drain systems should offer a high drainage capacity—not less than 42 liters/min in a normal hydrothermal room installation, and higher (minimum 60 liters/min) for other specific applications, such as experience showers. There should be an adequate fall to each drain (usually 1:100), and care should be taken to minimize the potential for user accidents (slip and trip). Typically, slip-resistant floor surfaces are required.

Drainage grids/grates may be lockable to both prevent vandalism and ensure large objects are not evacuated into the system. In addition, traps are required on drains to prevent smells from lingering inside the piping, and drainage systems can also be connected to recycling systems to minimize waste/water pollution and improve utility efficiencies.

Heating and Cooling Services

Giving the importance of hot and cold experiences in a hydrothermal spa, special attention must be paid to creating water and air that is of correct temperature. This can be especially challenging in regions where

Building a wet room requires specific expertise and careful planning.

Lighting plays an important role in the spa—the environment can be changed completely simply by changing the colors the lights are emitting.

cold water is not available—such as in the heat of the Middle East.

Many of the features in a hydrothermal spa require cooling down versus heating. For example, snow caves, ice fountains, cold plunge pools and spray-mist experience showers need to be chilled and cool. Depending on the location, chilled and/or cold water will either be provided by the mains or created on site. Conversely, hydrotherapy pools, onsen pools, tropical rain-shower experiences and many others are warm experiences and require heated water or air. The alternate hot-and-cool experience found in a Kneipp walk or Kneipp basin is an example of an experience that must supply both hot and chilled water at a specified temperature, in order to deliver the correct Kneipp experience.

In the Middle East and parts of Asia and Asia-Pacific, cold water is available via the mains, but it isn't usually "cold" by the time it reaches its destination. Chilled

water may be provided instead, but this water is usually contaminated with chemicals and, therefore, unusable. Experts are required to solve this dilemma, and they may introduce heat exchangers to cool down the "cold" water from the taps for use in fog showers, cold plunge pools, etc.

Lighting and Audio/Visual

Lighting and audio/visual add significantly to the ambience of hydrothermal cabins. Lighting for aesthetic purposes can be quite sophisticated and multi-dimensional, including changing colors and specialist effects. It's important to remember to provide lighting for cleaning and maintenance.

Light fixtures must be waterproof and robust and allow for easy maintenance like bulb changes.

Similarly, music and sound effects are used to create the required ambience. This means the provision of a programmable MP3 player/controller is required,

Specific Spa Functionality Required In a Building Management System:

- Acoustic sound off/on (music and alarm)
- Acoustic volume control (music and alarm)
- Activation signal (e.g., panic button)
- Maintenance issue alerts (e.g., light outages; water leakage; low levels in dosing system; etc.)
- Equipment off/on
- Fan speeds/air extraction rates
- Fault signal/message
- Lighting-level adjustment
- Set/monitor timers
- Room-temperature monitoring and adjusting
- Water/steam-temperature monitoring and adjusting
- Service reminders
- Password protection and restricted access
- Remote control access via Internet connection

together with waterproof speakers, resistant against both humidity and corrosion.

Newer developments in audio/visual include TV installations with specialist waterproof monitors and other broadcasting components.

Building Management Systems

Building Management Systems (BMS) allow control and monitoring of all the building services—including HVAC automation, energy control/consumption, access control, video surveillance, ventilation, security and fire protection—from a single point. In addition, they enable easier operation and maintenance of all functions of a building. In the case of hotel installations, a BMS is usually already in place and can be adapted to the spa environment.

Depending on its functionality, it should be possible to control and monitor temperature, lighting, music, etc., from a central screen at the reception desk; control panels should be in place throughout the spa to manage and maintain various equipment and

Building Management Systems allow for centralized and remote monitoring of all building services.

functions. These control panels gather relevant signals and alerts, routing them back to the central unit. Warnings/alerts can be issued when a light bulb has gone out, temperatures are above or below normal, a therapist or guest has pushed a panic button, water ingress/leakage is occurring, etc.

It's important to note there is a downside to remotely controlling thermal rooms and pool installations. If you take the need for physical checks out of these areas, there's a risk that problems in the system will go unrecognized/unseen. For example, there could be water leakage or even risk of fire that go unnoticed because no physical checks are being made.

There are standard rules and regulations (in fact, laws in many countries) that insist thermal cabins and pools be checked physically every six hours—in this case, the cabins are set to switch off every eight hours of operation, so that a physical check is guaranteed to be conducted and the experience turned back on. However, a BMS system can be programmed to override the physical check by simply turning the experience on remotely. To avoid this happening, a key switch or touch panel with a pin code should be positioned at the thermal room or pool itself, and it must be programmed not to re-start until a staff member has physically checked it.

Plant/Mechanical Rooms

One of the most common mistakes made in hydrothermal spa designs is the omission or poor planning of the size and location of the plant/mechanical room. And, of course, without the mechanics/equipment that runs the thermal and pool areas, they simply won't operate. This means much consideration should be given to the location and size of the plant rooms during the building design stage.

Expert input is necessary to understand plant/mechanical requirements of the various hydrothermal areas. In simple terms, a heated swimming pool will have a larger plant room than a salt cave, while a sauna or steam room's mechanics can either be located on the outside of the cabin, or in a plant room located a short distance from the cabin. All should be discreetly accessible by qualified personnel at all times.

Plant rooms have two important functions:

1. They house the major water, electrical and HVAC systems that support the thermal room or pool.

2. They offer access to equipment, e.g., dosing systems that require replenishment and maintenance, along with the major water, electrical, HVAC installations that support the entire installation.

Chapter Six

Health, Safety and Hygiene

Consideration for the health and wellbeing of users begins when a spa is in its earliest design stages. Whether building a residential or commercial spa facility, it's important to take into account the factors that affect the wellbeing, either directly or indirectly, of the people using the thermal cabins and pools.

The "health" of any building—regardless of usage—is something designers/architects have been becoming more and more aware of in recent years. In the case of hydrothermal builds, the most important health and safety factors are governed by the successful implementation of these core elements: heating, ventilation, air conditioning, building materials and cleaning agents.

By their very nature, hydrothermal areas, with their extensive use of heat and moisture, are ideal environments for the growth of fungus and mold— something that can be controlled during the design and building process and maintained through proper maintenance and cleaning. In addition, the high levels of moisture make the surfaces (floors and benches) incredibly conducive to slipping—another factor that is easily mitigated by using the correct materials.

The high, ambient temperatures used throughout the building to keep wet and minimally clothed bathers comfortable means that waterborne fungus and mold

High, ambient temperatures combined with large amounts of water means it's important to keep hydrothermal areas well cleaned and maintained.

isn't only an issue in the thermal cabins and pool areas—they can also surface in other communal and relaxation spaces.

In Design

Increasingly, more and more spa designers, owners and operators are actively engaged in the promotion and development of healthy buildings. They understand that it's important to be able to deliver the benefits of health and wellness treatments/experiences in a building that is specifically designed to be "healthy and well."

In the broadest sense, a "healthy building" is designed with the goal of reducing any negative impact it might have on occupants and the environment. That means using building materials and best practices that minimize risk to a person's health—whether that be through illness or accident.

During the design phase, it's imperative to consider and analyze the materials that will be used and to understand how they will withstand the effects of steam, sweat, oils and cleaning water/agents.

In thermal rooms and communal spaces, it's important to choose surfaces (benches, floors, walls) with minimal joints, thus avoiding the need for excess grouting. This makes cleaning and disinfecting easier, and, ultimately, longer lasting and requiring less maintenance. Additionally, specialist building materials, such as mortar-coated, expanded, polystyrene hard foam, make it possible to clad walls, floors, steps, benches and shelves in ways that are completely waterproof and mold-resistant. For example, in contrast to plasterboard, hard-foam polystyrene has been proven to prevent the formation of mold due to its alkaline properties. So usage of this humidity-resistant building board will minimize the risk of infection or allergies because it doesn't provide a suitable breeding ground for microscopic organisms or germs.

Continuous-surface loungers are easy for cleaning and maintenance.

Proper drainage planning is also imperative, as it plays a major role in the health of a hydrothermal building. All excess water used during treatments and in cabins and pools must have somewhere to go. Correct drainage keeps bacteria from breeding and also minimizes the slip risks caused by wet and dirty floors. (Not surprisingly, slipping and falling is the most common accident that can occur in a spa area).

Ventilation also plays a key factor in the health of the building and the health of those in it. In addition to the ventilation requirements outlined in chapter five (or page 79), it is essential to ensure smooth, not flexible, exhaust ducts are installed and that they fall in the direction of a drain point(s). This is imperative to avoid any pooling or lying of water in the ducting, preventing the incubation of legionella bacteria, the exposure to which can cause potentially fatal pneumonia. In cabins that are highly affected by heat, water and humidity, there should be a ventilated cavity between the room walls (or cladding) and the building walls.

Of course, cleaning and maintenance play a key role in minimizing health risks in any building. Wet and humid areas are difficult to clean and maintain at the best of times—in any building, the bathroom is the most susceptible to fungus and mold. This makes it vitally important to design the building/space while having the perspective of the person(s) who will clean it in mind. For example, consider creating rounded versus square corners for easier cleaning and always use sloped surfaces to avoid unhygienic pools of water on seats and other flat surfaces. Make sure there is an easy path for water and cleaning solutions to reach the drainage in the floor.

Emergency call systems, like those found in the healthcare industry, should be included in the design phase. These systems will alert staff to incidents or accidents, and, because all areas of a hydrothermal

Pool Water Safety

Pool staff should be trained to conduct regular testing of the pool water. Below are testing guidelines:

Daily Tests (Every 2-3 Hours)	Water Quality Values
Free Chlorine	Range 0.5 to 3.0 mg/l (Aim for 1.0 to 2.0 mg/l)
Combined Chlorine	Not more than one third of total chlorine
pH	Range 7.2 to max. 7.6 (Aim for 7.2 to 7.4)

Weekly Tests	Water Quality Values
Alkalinity	100 ppm to 180 ppm Sodium Hypochlorite 100 ppm to 120 ppm Calcium Hypochlorite
Calcium Hardness	200 ppm to 1000 ppm (not less than 200 ppm)
TDS	Total Dissolved Solids Max. 1000 ppm above source water
Pool Balance	Refer to Langelier Saturation Index

Pool Chemical Room Safety

Careful consideration has to be given for safe delivery of chemicals, including offloading and transfer within the building, avoiding stairs where possible.

Storage: Adequate, separate storage and containment space must be provided for the chemical containers and bags required for the normal daily and weekly refilling of the operational chemical day tanks.

Containment Bunds: A chemical bund area should be constructed in concrete with a cement render internally and finished with a chemical-resistant (or fiberglass-lined) material, providing a fully contained bund capable of holding 110% of the maximum chemical volume.

Segregation: Separate enclosures should be maintained for all potentially hazardous chemicals (acids and alkalis) in separately ventilated rooms, with a minimum of four air changes per hour.

Drench Showers/Eyewashes: Emergency drench showers/eyewashes are recommended in commercial chemical rooms.

Eyewash: A sealed sterile type of eyewash bottle should be located near the intake point and in the chemical stores

Sink: A large sink with hot and cold running water is required for cleaning the chemical injectors.

spa have associated risks, these systems should not only be adopted in the most "at risk" spaces (such as the thermal cabins and pool areas) but throughout the facility.

Key Design Considerations for Health/ Safety/Hygiene:

- Proper drainage to avoid excess water that can cause slips and/or breed bacteria

- Ventilation that enables the proper flow of oxygen and condensation

- Emergency call systems

- Measures for easy cleaning and disinfecting of all areas

- Building materials that minimize the growth of mold and bacteria

In Construction

Of course, the goal is that most risks are eliminated during the design stage. However, no matter how focused designers and architects are on these points, the construction phase is often where even the most conscientious professionals can see radical changes to their original specification. This is the phase when most changes are implemented, in particular, "value engineering"—where specified materials, equipment and services are modified or omitted in order to save money.

Often, during the design phase, clients are unwilling to agree to specified, branded products in tender documents and/or drawings. This means design intent can give way to financial pressure during the actual build. Product substitution is a frequent practice in the construction industry, and, though designers will reference a particular product or manufacturer, contracts will often carry the clause to allow for "or equal and approved" products. This invites contractors to offer financial incentives by providing products they feel are more competitively priced but often don't offer the same quality. And, of course, budget constraints means these "alternative" products are frequently accepted because they provide significant short-term cost reductions.

Common Mistakes

- Emergency call buttons in wet areas are designed to withstand heat and water. A wet area specialist will install them in thermal cabins and pool areas but they are not responsible for the entire call system which must be integrated by an M & E consultant.

- Leading with design and not considering safety/health

- Not allowing for disabled access and installing as an afterthough

- Forgetting slip-resistant flooring for wet area floors and multi-tier seating

- Cleaning tiled areas with pressure washers that end up blowing grout from the joints, creating bacteria and mold traps

- Not using heat resistant materials for handles in saunas

- Not ensuring that all doors to thermal cabins open out and have non-mechanical latching systems or heavy self-closing devices

- Incorrect ventilation causing poor air quality and/or condensation in ducting

Of course, this short-term financial gain can lead to the construction of substandard hydrothermal areas that quickly fall foul of health, safety and hygiene standards after construction.

In Operation

"Don't expect what you don't inspect!" is the best advice for spa operators. A clean and healthy environment in which guests can enjoy the facilities is the responsibility of the spa manager—whose job is to supervise the staff and ensure vital duties are performed at all levels.

Risk Assessment

In any business, there is the potential that a staff member or client can be injured or become ill as a result of an incident occurring in the workplace. This is why, whether it's a legal requirement or not, operators should carry out risk assessments on all aspects of their spas. Everything considered a potential risk should be fully documented. Further safeguards to assist operators in refuting or diminishing any claims that may occur: keeping thorough cleaning and maintenance records, as well as customer-usage numbers and chemical applications.

A risk assessment looks at the steps to be taken to eliminate and control risk and examines every possible "what if" scenario. There are online courses and organizations, such as the International Spa Association, that can help guide this process.

Risk Assessment Should Include the Following:

- Identification of all hazards (such as slippage, waterborne illnesses, chemical imbalances, etc.)

- Evaluation of the associated risks

- Consideration of the severity of the consequences and chances of it occurring

- Identification of all persons (including staff, contractors, guests) at risk

- Establish control measures to prevent risks

Identifying potential risks is the first step in ensuring safety in a hydrothermal spa area.

- Ensure staff and guests are aware of any potential risks and symptoms
- Identify specific legal duty or requirement relating to the risk

Control Measures to Consider:

Thermal Areas:

- Display clear instructions in prominent positions explaining how equipment should be used
- Minimize/eliminate potential for scalding or burning
- Ensure proper ventilation and drainage
- Conduct and document regular cleanings and checks—hourly, daily, weekly, monthly, yearly
- Test alarm systems regularly
- Always provide a supply of drinking water for guests and staff

Pool Areas:

- Display clear instructions about safe usage
- Follow a daily, weekly, monthly and yearly cleaning and maintenance routine
- Regularly test waters for disinfectant, pH levels and clarity
- Check filters and backwash as advised
- Drain and clean system as advised
- Ensure plant room and chemical storage area is well-ventilated
- Clearly label and store chemicals away from each other
- Follow applicable legal legislation for handling of chemicals

Wet Area Hygiene

Hygiene is important at every level of a spa—from pool water treatment and the correct design of ventilation ducts to the effective daily cleaning of floors and the deep cleaning of body fat residues from steam baths. This has a direct impact on the health and safety of the spa.

Major Health, Safety and Hygiene Risks:

- Accidental slipping due to poorly specified, cleaned or badly drained surfaces
- Bacterial cross-contamination from user to user
- Fatal waterborne illnesses, such as legionella
- Numerous illnesses, such as ear infections and viral conditions, transferred via poor pool water treatment and sanitizing

There are specially designed acidic cleaning solutions for tiles, fittings and accessories that will dissolve lime deposits and grease scum gently, while specialized pipeline disinfectants attack waterborne germs and fungus their its source.

Chapter Seven

Sustainability, Ecology and Economy

· ·

What was once thought of as "going green" has evolved from a passing trend into a long-term commitment to sustainability— the concept of making choices that have a positive impact on both people and the planet. Sustainability is all about looking towards the future when planning for today.

· ·

Sustainability means thinking about alternative sources of power, such as solar and wind power.

Spas by their very nature are inherently focused on personal/individual "sustainability" through health and wellness—everything a spa delivers is designed to help people live longer, better and more fulfilling lives.

Many spas embrace the concept of "green" or "sustainability" by closely scrutinizing the products they offer; reducing single-use supplies with durable beverage cups, cloth hand towels or microfiber body wraps; and simply asking clients to reduce the time spent in showers and to reduce the number of towels they use.

Of course, there's much more spas can do to positively affect the world in which we live. Considering sustainability during the planning and building stages of a hydrothermal spa area is not only good for the environment, but also good for the reputation of the industry, and, last but not least, will have a positive impact on the profitability of your spa.

Sustainable Materials/Products

Designing a wet area from the ground up provides the opportunity to think about integrating sustainability into every aspect of a hydrothermal spa. There are numerous ways to bring sustainability into the build—including conscious consideration of the building materials and products being used to construct the cabins and pools.

To minimize the impact on the environment, many providers and manufacturers to the hydrothermal industry have adopted "green" practices, including reducing the amount of emissions that are released into the atmosphere, using less raw materials, recycling waste material and extending the durability of their products. This last point is important, because, although the expense of sustainable and eco-friendly solutions is often greater at the offset, costs in the long run are typically much less.

The first step is to research the provenance of the materials and products that are being used to see if they follow the environmental ethos of your hydrothermal spa. For example, look at the woods chosen to build the sauna and/or banya—are they being sourced sustainably from managed forests? Are the tiles made of sustainable materials, and/or do the tile suppliers adopt eco-friendly practices throughout the manufacturing process? If you are sourcing an entire cabin, has it been designed and manufactured with sustainability at its core?

Since heat is such a huge part of a hydrothermal spa—and with heat comes the attendant drain on electrical and/or gas resources—it's imperative to pay close attention to insulation. Thermal insulation saves costs and energy by reducing the working hours of steam generators and heating; it also reduces the maintenance costs of this equipment. One of the most common (and, ultimately, most costly) mistakes a builder makes when constructing a thermal cabin is the use of materials that do not effectively hold heat

. . . .

Comparing Insulation Value of Common Building Materials

The lower the U-Value, the more optimal the insulation properties of the material; conversely, the higher the R-Value, the more optimal the Insulation properties

Wall Material	Thickness (MM)	U-Value (Low Value=Good)	R-Value* (High Value=Good)
Insulated Dry Wall	150	0.35	16.23
Concrete Blocks	200	0.39	14.6
Brick Wall	200	0.41	13.9
Poured Concrete	250	0.55	10.33
Coated Polystyrene Building Board	50	0,59	9.6

*R-Value is measurement used in USA

or withstand moisture. Building a sauna or a steam room with materials that are used throughout the rest of a building will likely result in rooms that are very costly to heat up—both in terms of cost to the environment and actual monetary expense to the operator. The insulation value—called "R-value" or "U-value," depending on the country of origin—of the materials being used is incredibly relevant. For example, common building materials, such as concrete blocks and plaster, have poor R-values and will suck up the heat before the cabin itself will heat up. A sauna using concrete blocks might take two hours to get to the correct temperature, while a sauna of the same size constructed using specialized insulation techniques and coated foam board will take just 20 minutes to get to temperature.

In a steam room, insulation is also important in water conservation—a properly insulated room will require less steam to be delivered to create the correct humidity levels.

As water is such a huge part of wet area spa builds, a particular focus must be put on all areas being waterproof and watertight. For example, if pools are included in the spa build, use materials that are proven to be the most effective at retaining water—such as stainless steel or composite GRP (fiberglass) versus cement. Water leakage is the biggest problem in pool builds but can be easily avoided by using the correct materials.

Ecological Solutions

Being in a position to use renewable energy—such as solar or wind power—for generating electricity to run a hydrothermal spa is the ultimate in putting sustainability first. If this is impossible, an affordable way to utilize solar power is to adopt solar-roof panels to heat water for the pools and showers. Ground source heat pumps, which harness natural ground heat by pumping water through underground pipes, require less electrical energy and are an extremely sustainable and effective method for heating and cooling water. Tankless or on-demand water heaters, which heat

Common Mistakes

- Not willing to commit to a bigger initial investment for the savings payoff in the long-term

- Uncontrolled usage/consumption of water

- Concrete is only a green material in its raw, base-component format, as all constituent parts are from the earth, but it is the production and transportation of concrete that causes all its green credentials to fall away.

- Building everything from scratch on site is not as green as the use of prefabricated structures, built in a factory with all waste materials harvested and disposed of ethically or recycled professionally. E.g., wood sawdust can be reused, wood offcuts can heat a sauna factory throughout the winter, expanded polystyrene offcuts are harvested in the factory and recycled into yogurt pots, etc.

- Just having "green" products is not enough for sustainability; owners and developers need to look at every element of spas from the ground up

- Water recycling is not just the job of infrastructure and utility providers—spas can do it to.

- Not harnessing air and heat energy used in the spa somewhere else—e.g., producing snow and ice creates a lot of heat; employ a heat exchanger to use that heat to add a few "free" degrees to the water being used for the vitality pool

Saving Energy

Energy consumption in thermal rooms varies greatly according to the method of construction and the selected finishes. The denser the material, the more energy it will take to heat the structure, rather than the bathing atmosphere.

For example, a concrete room with 20 mm-thick granite finishes will take an enormous amount of thermal energy to heat the structure before the room can be at bathing temperature; in colder climates this can take hours and cost a great deal of money to operate. Therefore, considering the thermal effectiveness of the building materials used is imperative.

Some examples from a simple steam room (steam output is measured in kilograms per hour (kg/hr) or pounds per hour (lbs/hr) are shown below:

- Concrete with granite finish requires 1.2 kg/hr of steam, equal to 0.9 kW in electrical load

- Insulated, coated foam boards with the same finish require 1.0 kg/hr of steam, equal to 0.75 kW in electrical load

- In simple terms, the energy used by a concrete/granite room will be 20% greater and, therefore, cost 20% more to run.

- Given that the average life of a steam room is at least 10 years and often a lot more, the low cost of "traditional" building materials at the outset may reduce the capital costs of the project, but the ongoing higher revenue costs of inefficient construction will last the life of the steam room and far outweigh the initial saving.

water as needed versus a water heater that features a continuous heating source, are another option, but, because the water flow rate is not likely to meet the needs of guests in a large spa, these might be better to supplement other heating solutions. And, if there's an option to use an electricity or gas supplier that provides green-sourced energy, you can be "green" with minimal effort and outlay of cash.

Of course, making and supplying your own energy is, more often than not, cost-prohibitive. In this case, it's important to focus on other ways to save on energy waste by using appliances that are rated energy efficient (e.g., the Energy Star rating). And, although people are becoming more conscious of energy conservation, relying on staff and guests to shut off lights when not in use is not enough; instead, consider installing sensors that will dim or shut lights off completely in unused areas of the spa.

A simple way to manage water waste is by installing similar sensors on faucets and showers so that water is never left running. Showers can also be programmed to shut off after a certain amount of time to minimize waste. Low-flow toilets should always be used; additionally, look to recover water wherever possible for reuse. For example, avoid using detergents in the shower areas so the water is re-treatable and re-useable.

If the hydrothermal spa is in an area that benefits from large amounts of rainwater, explore a rainwater-harvesting system that will collect and filter rainwater for use around the spa.

Getting the ventilation and climate control correct in the pool area will pay off in the long run by combating evaporation—another huge water waster.

Sourcing products for the hydrothermal area that are eco-friendly throughout their lifecycle minimizes waste in the long run. A good example of this can be found in today's choice of steam generators. Steam generators that are designed with eco-principles tend to cost more initially but can last up to 20 years versus a more affordable model that may last only three years. The implications on the environment are numerous. The cheaper unit will be sealed so repairs are impossible—

Sourcing wood for saunas from a managed forest environment is good practice.

which means it ultimately ends up in the landfill and a new unit must be purchased, while the more expensive steam generator allows for both repair and recycling.

Economic Advantages

The economic advantages to building a sustainable and eco-friendly hydrothermal spa are numerous. Up-front investments in sustainable designs and technology promise to deliver financial paybacks over the life of the building in the form of lower utility bills and reduced operating and maintenance costs.

Another less obvious, but equally important, benefit is the goodwill created by these initiatives with both the local community and guests. Everyone wants to be part of an ethos that encourages sustainability and eco-friendly practices. In short, creating a sustainable and green hydrothermal spa can provide unique marketing opportunities.

Explore sustainability strategies with your team to save money in the long run!

Resources

Use these resources to make your spa "greener":

- **Green Spa Network**
  www.greenspanetwork.org
  Sustainability assessments and easily adoptable practices for spas

- **Green Globe 21**
  www.greenglobe.com
  Certification for the sustainable operations and management of travel and tourism companies and their related supplier businesses

- **LEED (Leadership in Energy & Environmental Design)**
  www.usgbc.org/leed
  LEED certification is recognized across the globe as the premier mark of achievement in green building

In Conclusion

The contents of this book reflect numerous sources of information on wet area design and construction. As noted in the introduction, this is not an exhaustive resource but a starting point.

The goal of the publisher and author was to communicate the extensive benefits of hydrothermal bathing rituals—including detoxification, an improved immune system and the management of high blood pressure—and the important role these experiences play in today's modern spa builds.

We wanted to give readers a tool to help steer the process of designing and building wet areas that are not only user-friendly and health-transformative but that deliver a long-term, positive return on investment for spa operators.

Resources

Websites are an excellent resource for information on spas and wet spa areas.

Associations

A worldwide list of spa & wellness associations can be found here:
www.globalspaandwellnesssummit.org/index.php/spa-industry-resource/associations

Publications

A comprehensive list of magazines and books can be found here:
www.globalspaandwellnesssummit.org/index.php/spa-industry-resource/publications

Spa Standards by Country

Links to a long list of spa standards can be found here:
http://www.globalspaandwellnesssummit.org/index.php/spa-industry-resource/standards-and-practices

Hydrothermal Codes and Standards

The following are codes and standards that are often referred to by wet area specialists:

- Americans with Disabilities Act; www.ada.gov
- German Sauna Standards; www.ral-guetezeichen.de
- German DIN 19643-4; www.beuth.de
- German DIN 51097; www.beuth.de
- Leadership in Energy & Environmental Design (LEED); www.usgbc.org/leed
- Pool Water Treatment Advisory Group (PWTAG); www.pwtag.org
- Trade Rules of the Swedish Ceramic Tile Council; www.bkr.se
- Charted Institute for the Management of Sport and Physical Activity (CIMSPA); www.cimspa.co.uk
- International Building Codes; www.iccsafe.org
- ÖNORM M6219 Austrian standards; ww.bdb.at

Glossary

Aromatherapy

The use of aromatic plant extracts and essential oils in massage, baths, showers and thermal cabins

Aquathermal bathing (synonym "hydrothermal bathing")

Pertaining to the temperature effects of water used in thermal cabins and pools (Origin Greek)

Arctic ice Room

Operating at 1° C to 4° C,, these rooms provide contrast therapy to the hot rooms in a spa and mimic the traditional experience of a "roll in the snow"

Balnea/Balneum

Smaller version of a Roman thermae (bathhouse) found in ancient Rome (Origin Latin)

Balneotherapy

General term for water-based treatments using natural thermal, spring, mineral or seawater to induce relaxation, improve the circulation, stimulate the immune system and bring about detoxification (Origin Latin)

Banya/Banja

Term originally meant "bathhouse" in Russia but has been adopted to refer to the specific sauna-like room in a Russian bathhouse. (Origin Russia)

Biosauna (or Soft Sauna)

A gentler, less extreme version of a Finnish sauna operating at 50° C to 60° C

Caldarium/Caldaria

The hottest room in ancient Roman baths and a precursor to today's steam bath (Origin Latin)

Contrast Therapy

Refers to the therapeutic effects of hot and cold temperatures

Experience Showers

Multi-sensory shower experiences incorporating smell, sound and visual effects

Finnish Sauna

A wood structure with a heat source (wood-burning, electric or gas); the hottest and driest room in any spa, running at 80° C to 105° C

Floatation Bath

A warm bath containing oils or salts, where the client floats on the water, usually in the dark or in subdued lighting. A floatation tank is bed-sized and is a closed environment, often in total darkness.

Foot Spa

Specifically designed for bathing feet in cool or warm water in between hot treatments; feet play an important role in the heating and cooling process of the body due to the small amount of flesh and fat on them

Frigidarium/Frigidaria

The cold plunge pool in ancient Roman baths (Origin Latin)

Furo

A private bathing ritual in Japan that takes place in a bath made of wood; the furo is often found in private homes (Origin Japan)

Hamam

The word "hamam" literally translates to "bathroom" in Turkish and refers to the entire Turkish bathhouse. A Turkish hamam is a large domed structure with a central room (sikaklek) in which the belly stone (göbek tasi) takes center stage. The belly stone is traditionally where attendants scrub and clean bathers. (Origin Turkish)

Hammam

A Moroccan hammam is similar to a Turkish bath but has retained more of the traditional Roman bathing ritual—sending the bather on a journey through smaller chambers with varying temperatures (like the Roman journey through the laconium, caldarium, frigidarium and tepidarium). (Origin Moroccan/N. African)

Hot Tub

Large tub or small pool of heated water used for hydrotherapy or pleasure. Some have jets for massage purposes. Hot tubs are sometimes known as spas or by the trade name Jacuzzi.

Hydrotherapy

The use of water for pain relief and treatment. The therapeutic effect of water depends on the temperature, depth and duration of immersion and its mineral content to soothe painful muscles and joints, as well as stimulate the circulation and immune system.

Hydrothermal Bathing

Pertaining to the temperature effects of water used in thermal cabins and pools

Ice Cave/igloo

Operating at 7° C to 15° C, these rooms provide contrast therapy to the hot rooms in a spa and mimic the traditional experience of a "roll in the snow."

Ice Fountain

An access of ice in a spa for bathers to cool their bodies between hot treatments

Infrared Therapy

Using long-wave infrared radiation to distribute warmth through the peripheral nervous system

Inhalation Room

Specific treatment room for inhaling agents to treat respiratory conditions such as asthma, bronchitis and emphysema

Jacuzzi

Named after inventor and manufacturer, this is a bath or pool large enough for several persons sitting down to be massaged by underwater jets.

Kneipp Therapy

A 19th century adaptation of hydrotherapy formulated by Pastor Sebastian Kneipp (1821-1897) and consisting of hot and cold water treatments, walking barefoot in the morning dew, and the use of herbal bath oils, all combined with physical exercise and a diet of natural food. Popular in Austria, Germany and Switzerland.

Laconium

Name originates from Roman baths; this is a warm room (38-42 °C) where bathers can relax for long periods of time on benches or in individual, heated loungers or chairs. (Origin Latin)

Lap Pool

An exercise pool used for swimming lengths/laps and is commonly 25 m long x 12.5 m wide x 1.5 m deep. You can also find pools that offer both resistance and lap swimming in smaller spaces with the aid of motorized water-flow mechanisms.

Mineral Water

Water of natural purity used for bathing and/or drinking, the source of which has to be in a subterranean and protected water deposit. Mineral waters can have an acidic, basic or neutral pH, depending on the types of dissolved solids in the water. Depending on use, the content of some substances must not exceed the indicated limits.

Mud Bathing

Mud bathing originated thousands of years ago as a medicinal and beautifying ritual. The body is coated with organic thermal mud, and, depending on the minerals inherent in the mud, they can cleanse, exfoliate, absorb toxins, increase circulation and soften the skin.

Onsen

This pool type originates from Japan and has a significant role in the country's ritual bathing practices. "Onsen" translates as "hot springs" in Japanese and has come to refer to the natural spring baths found throughout

Japan. Their benefits are closely dependent on the mineral properties and content of the water itself and typically include the easing of neuralgia, alleviation of muscle pain, the reduction of the symptoms of chronic skin disease and the relief of chronic fatigue and stress. (Origin Japan)

Pestemal

A pestemal (pesh-te-mahl) is the authentic Turkish bath towel. It is flat-woven with hand-tied fringe, typically made of Turkish cotton, linen or even silk. It is also known as a hamam towel, as it is an essential element of the legendary Turkish bath experience. Pestemals come in countless designs, textures, weights and colors. The hand-towel version of the pestemal is called a peskir (pesh-kir).

Plunge Pool

A cold plunge pool, also traditionally known as a frigidarium, is a cold-water pool that is typically entered after and between hot thermal treatments to cool bathers down.

Refugium

The refugium is a relaxation area in a spa, typically smaller and more intimate than the tepidarium, and used for rest and sleeping.

Respiratory Therapy

The goal of respiratory therapy (also called inhalation therapy) is to improve respiration by steam inhalation combined with essential oils. There are specific treatments targeted at chronic conditions such as asthma, bronchitis and emphysema.

Salt Room/Cave

Salt therapy originated in Europe with natural salt caves and caverns. Claimed to relieve asthma, improve circulation and lower blood pressure, salt rooms and caves are specific treatment rooms requiring dry conditions, good ventilation and copious amounts of salt on the floor, walls and ceiling.

Sauna

There are several different styles of saunas in use today. The traditional and most common are Finnish saunas and Russian banyas; others include bio and infrared saunas. While various sauna types all run at slightly different temperatures and humidity, they are closely related in style, usage and health benefits.

Scotch Hose

An invigorating water jet massage that uses variable temperatures and pressure levels to stimulate circulation and relax muscles. Also known as the Scotch Hose Shower and Jet Blitz.

Sento

The Japanese developed a form of steam bath called the sento, a type of vapor bath that uses aromatherapy elements and includes body scrubbing. (Origin Japan)

Shower/Waterfall

Several shower options are available: cold waterfalls, mists, body jets and dramatic "experience showers" offering multi-sensory experiences that incorporate smells, sound and visual effects.

Snow Cavern

Cold rooms that use modern techniques to create real snow with which to cool the body. Operating at 1° C to 4° C, these rooms are becoming increasingly common in modern spas.

Spa Suite

A bedroom suite that offers additional spa equipment, such as a hot tub, treatment table, experience shower, etc.

Steam Bath/Room

The modern steam bath is unique in that it reaches 100% relative humidity—which gives it the element of steam/fog. The caldarium is the Roman precursor to the steam bath (also commonly called steam room).

Steam Shower

A steam shower is a type of bathing where a humidifying steam generator produces water vapor that is dispersed around a person's body. A steam shower is essentially a small steam room that offers the typical features of a bathroom shower, often with a seat for comfort.

Sudatorium

A type of steam room in a Roman bath where the high temperature promotes sweating.

Swiss Shower

A shower in which jets of water are sprayed onto the body from above, and also from numerous nozzles on the side.

Temazcal

The temazcal, or "sweat lodge," is another example of thermal bathing. (Origin Mexico)

Tepidarium/Tepidaria

Relaxation spaces with loungers and beds; the Romans called these areas the tepidarium

Thalasso/Thalassotherapy

From the Greek word thalassa, meaning "sea," it is the medical use of seawater as a form of therapy for preventive or curative purposes. The term includes seaweed, algae wraps and hydrotherapy.

Thermae/Therma

In Roman times, the thermae, from the Greek word thermos, meaning "hot," were facilities for bathing; the term usually refers to the large public bathing complexes. Most Roman cities had at least one such building, which were centers not only for bathing, but socializing. (Origin Latin)

Thermal Bathing

Thermal bathing is commonly associated with naturally hot water, rich in mineral salts, iodine and gases. The place is often referred to as a spa, which is traditionally used to mean a place where the water is believed to have special health-giving properties.

Thermal Suite

The collection of thermal treatments in a spa is commonly called the thermal suite.

Vichy Shower

A Vichy shower is a horizontal series of showerheads forming a "rain bar" over a waterproof, cushioned treatment table.

Vitality Pool

A vitality pool is the generic name for what people commonly refer to as a "Jacuzzi" (the brand name that has become synonymous with pools with water jets). Vitality pools offer a mini-hydrotherapy experience.

Water Cure

The use of water as a form of physical therapy, e.g., the Kneipp walk, which uses a mix of hot and cold water to stimulate the circulation of blood. Pebbles on the bottom of the stream/walkway massage the feet and the alternation of hot and cold baths stimulate circulation to all parts of the body.

Watsu®

These are pools designed specifically for Watsu massage, a gentle form of body therapy performed in warm water.

Whirlpool Tub

This is a bath large enough for several persons sitting down to be massaged by underwater jets.

Index

Photo Credits

courtesy of Absolute Pool & Spa; 92

courtesy of Aria Resort & Casino; 49

courtesy of Barr + Wray Ltd.; X; 3; 7 (bottom); 11 (top); 18; 19; 32; 47; 56; 59; 61; 63; 71; 76; 88; 89; 90

courtesy of Center Parcs UK; Woburn Forest Location; 37; 50; 67

courtesy of Design For Leisure Ltd.; 5; 16; 41; 81

courtesy of Gharieni Group; 8 (bottom); 39; 51

courtesy of HygroMatik GmbH CSA; 6 (top and bottom); 26; 28; 30

courtesy of Kemitron GmbH; 9 (middle); 45

courtesy of Klafs GmbH & Co. KG; 11 (bottom); 23; 32; 44

courtesy of Lux Elements GmbH; 38; 55

courtesy of Nordic Spa-Nature, Quebec, Canada; 64

courtesy of Peninsula Hot Springs, Victoria, Australia; 65

courtesy of Ron Starr; 8 (top); 36

courtesy of Sommerhuber; 93

courtesy of THERMARIUM Bäder-Bau GmbH; 2; 7 (top); 11 (middle); 22; 25; 27; 31; 34; 43; 78; 87

courtesy of Tschuggen Hotel Group, Switzerland; 10 (bottom); 42; 60; 66; 68

courtesy of Two Bunch Palms; 7 (middle)

courtesy of Unbescheiden GmbH; 9 (bottom); 10 (top and middle); 52; 53

courtesy of WDT Werner Dosiertechnik GmbH & Co. KG; 9 (top); 46; 47; 48; 85

A special thanks to all the knowledgeable hydrothermal experts at the following companies:

absolute-pools: www.absolute-pools.com
Bringing pools to life through innovation, good design and industry best practice

Barr + Wray Ltd.: www.barrandwray.com
Spa interior design, engineering consultancy; and pool and thermal installation and maintenance

Design For Leisure Ltd.: www.designforleisure.com
Hydrothermal spa design consultants and implementation specialists

Gharieni Group: www.gharieni.com
German manufacturer of high-end spa tables and equipment

Hilton Worldwide: www.hiltonworldwide.com
One of the largest hospitality companies in the world

HygroMatik GmbH: www.hygromatik.de
A leading manufacturer of professional humidifiers and steam bath generators

Klafs GmbH & Co.: www.klafs.com
A market leader for sauna, spa and wellness with over 80 years experience

Kemitron GmbH: www.kemitron.com
Producer of fragrance, cosmetics, dosing pumps and process control systems for the spa and wellness industry

Lux Elements GmbH: www.luxelements.com
Specialist in producing hard foam, ready-to-tile, shaped elements for spa facilities

Six Senses Hotels Resorts Spas: www.sixsenses.com
Offering a layered approach that unites a pioneering spirit with treatments that go beyond ordinary

Sommerhuber – www.sommerhuber.com
Manufacturer of large-area heat storage ceramics focused on design and hygiene

THERMARIUM Bäder-Bau GmbH: www.thermarium.com
A single source for spa design, manufacturing, consulting and engineering

Unbescheiden GmbH: www.unbescheiden.com
Manufacturer of spa and hydrotherapy equipment since 1869

WDT Werner Dosiertechnik GmbH & Co. KG: www.werner-dosiertechnik.de
Control and dosing systems for swimming pools and wellness facilities